Africa: Through a Mirror

AFRICA

THROUGH A MIRROR

We Have a Continent to Build

SAIKOU CAMARA

Library of Congress Control Number: 2019908453

ISBNs: 978-0-9998296-4-6 (paperback); 978-0-9998296-5-3 (ePub); 978-0-9998296-6-0 (Kindle)

Printed in the United States
First Printing 2019

Jollof Publishing

To order, visit www.amazon.com

Dedication

My profound faith and believe in the destiny of our continent does not lie in the political class. I believe in the everyday working-class men and women of the African continent and I am hereby dedicating this book to them.

To the young men with low income jobs supporting their extended families; to the young single mothers struggling financially with their kid(s) and waking up every morning laboring to sustain their families; to the hardworking civil servants who got passed over for well deserving promotions at their places of employment once again due to government bureaucracies, corruption, and nepotism; to the young college students who are struggling with tuition and contemplating quitting; to the young journalists and human rights activists who risk arbitrary arrests and violent retribution in search of truth and justice; to the young people who are wandering around with hopelessness and risking their lives in cold and bottomless waters in search of greener pastures; and finally to the everyday underrepresented working African women who remain as loyal as they are dedicated daughters of our continent even when the continent has been unkind and unfair to them.

I want you to know that I hear your silent calls for help, your agonizing pains in isolation, and your relentless and continuous pursuit for prosperity. The struggle is part of the process. I see you. And I'm confident that God sees you too. Our strength is in our collective and your chances of success today are far higher than failure, but God only helps those who help themselves, you must arm yourselves. Arm yourselves with knowledge, good thoughts, good character traits, and the courage to persevere through difficult times. I believe in you and I trust that together we have a continent to build.

Affably Yours
—Saikou Camara

Dedication

Contents

Foreword

Saikou Camara does a magnificent job in holding post-independence Africa up to the mirror of time.

The reflection is not pretty, as it shows so many wrong turns. However, the nature of the human condition is that we learn from our mistakes.

I am truly thankful for the extent and depth of this review which is factual and without sentiment.

The major tragedy that it exposes is our almost total dependence on our previous colonizers for ideas and systems of how to govern and prosper in an industrialized society.

This review focuses on what has taken place in Africa. However, what takes place in Africa is often orchestrated by forces outside Africa such as multinational corporations, former colonial governments, the IMF, the World Bank, the WTO and the globalization of capital.

Despite the realistic accounting and analysis of the political and social history of the last 60 years the conclusions are hopeful as Africa has the human, land and mineral resources to build a continent.

This is a passionate call to all people of African descent to assume some responsibility in carrying forward the legacies of our Pan-African leaders inside and outside the continent. We must look inward to find the self-reliant solutions to the problems that we face.

I agree with Saikou, we do have a continent to build. We can only achieve this through unity, knowledge of our history and culture, self-determination, and by taking full responsibility for our actions.

The vision of economic freedom and the renaissance of African Civilization must be our consuming focus for the 21st century.

I recommend this book and hope that it finds a ready response in the hearts and minds of Africans and people of African descent everywhere.

Africa for the Africans, those at home and those abroad.

—Julius W. Garvey, M.D.
Associate Professor of Surgery
Albert Einstein College of Medicine

Preface

Why Africa?

Why me, Why you, Why us?

*"There is just no sense in pondering the functions of literature
without relating it to the actual society that uses it, to the centers of power within that society, and to the institutions that
mediate between literature and people."*

—RICHARD OHMANN

Chinua Achebe in his essay, *The Novelist as a Teacher* (1965), addresses crucial issues relating to the role of an African writer towards his/her society. Achebe assert-ed that *"the (African) writer cannot be excused from the task of re-education and re-generation that must be done."* The Af-rican writer has three primary functions in relation to his society as outlined by Achebe: 1. as a historian rescuing its past, 2. as a critic analyzing its present, and 3. as a mentor helping to guide it towards its future. Meaning it is a moral responsibility and even a duty for the African writer to be accountable for his/her society.

I am part of a forward-thinking African generation in which our former oppressors tell us to *"get over things"*;

perhaps in an attempt for us to accept the stagnated and beleaguered status quo of the African continent. We do not want to get over things anymore without understanding why they are the way they are. We deserve explanations if nothing else. How can we move on without knowing what we are moving away from?

Unless we examine, analyze and understand our problems, I do not think we can resolve them. The most fundamental aggression and harm we can commit against ourselves as Africans is to remain ignorant and not having the courage and fortitude to examine our lives' difficulties with honesty and sincerity. The plight of Africans begs for endless questions;

- Why did Europeans enslave Africans in the name of Christianity? Did Jesus not die for African sins?
- Why did Europeans colonize Africa when Africa is almost an island, it's only connection to the nearest land being the tiny Sinai Peninsula in Egypt?
- Why is Africa the poorest continent in the world when some of the largest, and richest, mineral deposits have been found in the continent of Africa? That does not make any sense. None of this makes any sense.
- Why do Africans keep voting in elections when African presidents scarcely lose elections?
- Why do African presidents own private jets when their countrymen are still hungry? Greed, heartlessness, wickedness, unscrupulousness, greed, greed, more greed!
- Why do African people settle their scores with civil wars instead of civil words? There are wars and rumors of war ringing from every corner of the continent.

We consider peaceful options only after exhausting violent ones.

- Why are we researching cure for diseases, but are not researching solutions for poverty, hunger, and wars (homicide and genocide)? Burundi, Liberia, Sierra Leone, Angola, Rwanda, Uganda, just to ring a bell.
- Why don't many children in Africa get the opportunity to go to school? If you grew up in West Africa, for example, you'd have only had a one-in-three chance of primary/elementary school education.
- Why has Africa, the motherland, fallen behind in terms of civilization when it is believed to be home of the human species, dating as far back as some 5 million years?
- Why is malaria, a disease that is both preventable and curable, one of the leading causes of death in Africa?
- Why are Africans still thirsty when the Nile is the longest river in the world flowing through Uganda, Ethiopia, Sudan and Egypt? If all the bends in the river were straightened out, it would flow from the Equator right up to the Scottish Highlands.
- Why are the children of Malawi still hungry when Lake Malawi in Southern Africa is home to around 500 different types of fish? That's more than anywhere else in the world.
- Why is Mogadishu, Somalia listed as the world's most dangerous city when more people die in America to gun violence than anywhere else in the world?
- Why is Cape Town among the top five most dangerous cities in the world? Yet, the only street in the world to house two Nobel Peace prize winners is in Soweto (Johannesburg), South Africa, Nelson Mandela

and Archbishop Desmond Tutu both have houses on Vilakazi Street.

- Why is Africa termed the Dark Continent? The amount of sunlight we are endowed with is unmatched anywhere else in the world.
- Why are African women constantly brutally battered when they are the most submissive women on earth? Not to say that I agreed with the notion that (African) women should be submissive to their male partners.
- Why has the war in the Democratic Republic of Congo gone almost unnoticed even though it is the largest and deadliest war in modern day African history? More than five million deaths are recorded between 1998 and 2008 and counting; the most lethal war since World War II.

I am not trying to instigate an aura of self-mutilation or humiliation; my only goal is to reflect on the state of the African continent.

Having asked these questions, I embarked on a research seeking for answers to these issues that seem peculiar to Africa. I understand that every civilization at some point in their struggles had to make conscious decisions regarding what they want and need as a people.

I am very well aware of the simple fact that Africa had gone through some of the worst dehumanization in human history. Africa has been the most humiliated and insulted continent in the world. Our very claim to humanity has been questioned at various times through history, our humanity abused, and our dignity insulted. These things have happened in the past and have gone on happening today. Slavery had weakened the human capital of the continent.

Colonialism has since long ago depleted the natural resources of the continent. And additionally, unfair trade deals, which are sometimes motivated by racism, continue to adulterate the continent.

I am also aware of the simple fact that Africa is not a single country, vis-à-vis the Berlin conference, but rather a composition of multiple nations (54 countries to be precise) with an array of troubles that are far from monolithic. Equally, I'm also aware of the economic disparity between Saharan (Arabs) and Sub-Saharan African (Black Africans) countries. And there is no doubt that Africa bears a heavy burden of epidemic disease outbreaks; be it polio, malaria, HIV and AIDS, Ebola, or yellow fever, and so on, and other natural disasters such as drought, floods, and desertification. All of these unfortunate events are crimes and misfortune incidents committed against the African continent, directly or otherwise, by foreign invaders or natural calamities.

By no means, however, should this literature be mistaken as though it is excusing the crimes committed against the African continent. This literature is compiled, despite the aforementioned disastrous occurrences, to instead attempt to examine our own actions as Africans that are detrimental to our growth and to our continent.

Chapter One

Introduction:
After 50 Years of Independence:

"To be frank, Africa was prepared for its independence…in just about the worst possible way. The last 50 years included civil wars, dictatorship, and corruption and so on"
—Howard French tells on NPR's September 26, 2010

In 1884 a congress was held in Berlin for the competing colonial governments to settle their disputes for territory in Africa. During the gathering, they declared that they were all determined to get their share of the *"magnificent African cake"*. The event was graced by self-declared partitionists at the time; the French, the Germans, the English, the Belgians, the Italians, the Dutch, the Portuguese, the Spaniards, the Swedes, as well as the Americans were all in attendance. They, in their wisdom or lack thereof, invited all necessary stakeholders except for the Africans. This gathering was perhaps the single biggest betrayal towards Africa in the history of this beautiful continent. There, the so-called partitionists sliced and diced our continent into bits and pieces. They sent their disciples into the continent, with Bibles in their pockets and rifles in their hands. They were determined and eager to steal, kill, rape, murder, or do whatever it may take to subdue the Africans to their commands. They premeditated their actions to commit crimes against Africa. Either black Africans will accept their propositions with the help of the Bible, or they will put the fear of God in them using the rifle, should that be necessary. Africans must accept their proposition (masked under Christianity) and pay taxes to their new colonial masters or die horrible deaths in the name of Christ.

By no means is this an attack on Christianity, matter of fact, as an African Muslim, I am hereby stating on record that it is the Middle Eastern Arabs under the mask of Islam who architected this horrific crime that the western countries learned from. It was the Arabs who first enslaved Africans. They murdered and tortured our people to become submissive and subdued to the teaching of the jihadists. These are some very uncomfortable truths, but they are facts that need to be stated.

After many years of this inglorious injustice in the name of God (as they proclaimed), by no choice of their own, the Europeans were forced to leave and render Africa her independence. But before they left, they made sure that Africa was organized and enclosed in an economy controlled by western imperialism. And today, that project is still in full effect.

Post-independence African leaders gathered in Addis Ababa, Ethiopia, under the invitation of King Haile Selassie in the year Nineteen Hundred and Sixty-Three (1963) *to discuss the fate of the continent.* There, Kwame Nkrumah, the then leader of Ghana, yielded to his fellow African leaders to integrate their disfranchised small countries into one Africa. He asked them to unite their economic resources and political agendas as one. He advised that if they fail to unite, they will henceforth all remain weak and irrelevant in global matters. Abban Eban, a former diplomat of Israel was once quoted saying, *"The Arabs never miss an opportunity to miss an opportunity."* I will also echo Abban's sentiments that *Africa never misses an opportunity to miss an opportunity*. Unfortunately, Nkrumah failed to convince his comrades to unite as one Africa. That was a huge missed opportunity for the continent. The continent that was once augured with a new era of prosperity and free of colonial interference soon went into political and economic collapses. Our leaders once hailed as liberators soon curdled into petty and benevolent corrupt dictators. As Nigerians would say, *who bewitched us*?

It has been over 50 years since majority of African countries celebrated independence from the crude colonial rule of our various colonial masters. The question that many Africans asked themselves is, is Africa truly independent today? Some will argue that a continent that is struggling to feed its population cannot pride itself with independence. If the critics are right, then the right question to ask is will Africa ever be truly independent?

Of what significance is our independence when we are still struggling with basic needs such as food and water? Our continent is still struggling to feed itself. The foods we eat are imported from abroad. Quality basic primary education is still a luxury within the continent that only a few can afford. Our economies cannot provide sustainable employment for citizens. Energy (electricity) is still scarce within the continent, non-existent in most regions. We are still struggling to provide basic healthcare for our citizens. Our people lost their African pride. We are no strangers to wars, corrupt officials, famine, dictatorships, raping of our young women, diseases, poor economic conditions and many other forms of human disasters.

It seems like the entire continent is in disarray and our young people are desperate for survival. Al Shabaab terror groups are terrorizing in East Africa, Boko Haram terror groups are terrorizing in West Africa, Human Traffickers and kidnappers are kidnapping and selling (enslaving) our young black migrants in North Africa, and Xenophobia is devastating migrants in South Africa. The young people of the continent are wandering in hopelessness and haplessness.

Was this what Jomo Kenyatta of Kenya, Kwame Nkrumah of Ghana, Sekou Toure of Guinea Conakry, Julius Nyerere of Tanzania, Amilcar Cabral of Cape Verde, Kenneth Kaunda of Zambia, Nelson Mandela of South Africa, Haile Selassie of Ethiopia, Edward Francis Small of The Gambia, Patrice Lumumba of Congo, and so many other inaugural African leaders who fought for self-rule within the continent had in mind? Will they be proud of us if they were here today? Perhaps those who fought for independence had a different idea of what they hope self-rule would bring to us. If the answer is yes, then it appears that we have all betrayed our continent.

When our inaugural leaders took over the continent and freed our people from colonialism, there was so much enthusiasm and optimism throughout the continent. Our people were hopeful that we would make it to the Promised Land by now. Today, the majority of the young masses seem to appreciate the countries of the children of our colonial masters more than our independent African countries. Just visit any foreign embassy in any African country and you would agree with me that almost every young African wants to get out of our continent. This begs the question: What went wrong? Many experts agree that Africa is still suffering from the post-traumatic syndromes of slavery and colonialism.

In 2002, Prime Minister Tony Blair described Africa as a *"blot on the world's conscience"*. There should be no doubt in anyone's mind that the world has wronged Africa. This has been well documented; though some may argue that it is under-documented. One thing that I am certain of is that there is very little to no chance that Tony Blair, his or any subsequent government, and the rest of the world will be cleaning that stain anytime soon. What concerns me is whether Africa is a stain on its own conscience. And if so, what have we done and what are we doing to clean that stain off our conscience? The stain on the world's conscience is the demon the world has to deal with, but what we can clean is the stain we have on our own conscience.

As an African with western education, I have heard both sides of the story about my people. I am more confused today as a college graduate than I was before I could read or write. The history books in Africa taught me that European and Arab merchants captured and enslaved my ancestors. On the contrary the history books of the western world taught me that my ancestors betrayed one another and sold out their own into slavery. No matter who did the capturing or selling of slaves, does this make it right or any less wrong? The morally correct response will be a *'no'*, but that is beside the point.

When I began compiling this literature, I was going

to express my disdain for slavery, how it had affected us post-independence, and all the other injustices dished out to my people. But in the middle of my 'brainstorming yoga' I couldn't help but keep thinking to myself, for how long will we wallow in anger and self-pity? When are we going to take responsibility for our own actions and employ corrective measures? Do not mistake this as asking us to forget the injustice that was meted against us. Rather, we must re-examine and reflect on our own self-destructive behaviors that continue to hinder our growth as a continent.

I am from The Gambia, West Africa, the smallest country on mainland Africa and among the poorest countries in the world. The Gambia, however, is the birthplace of Kunta Kinteh, arguably the most famous person ever to be forced into slavery out of Africa. Kunta gained his fame from his relentless fight against insurmountable odds to remain a free man. He was captured into slavery while fetching firewood in the outskirt of his village in rural Gambia, forced onto a slave ship along with hundred other young men and women for a grueling 4 months' voyage across the Atlantic Ocean, and sold as a *"slave"* at a Slave market in Annapolis, Maryland. After multiple reported attempts to escape from his slave masters, Kunta was brutally beaten and eventually mutilated to be subdued and succumbed to being enslaved but until his death in 1822 never for once considered himself a slave. Today I sit in my centralized air-conditioned apartment, in the same land some of my ancestors were brought in as slaves. I attempted to cheat my conscience by trying to blame the rest of the world for all of Africa's problems. However, my morale and conscience would not let me forfeit our collective responsibility as Africans.

In my inaugural book, *"Testimony of an African Immigrant"*, I asked these same questions, why am I in America today? Why are my countrymen risking their lives by getting on canoes and fishing boats trying to sail their way across Oceans into Europe? Why were my countrymen in the early 1990's hiding in cargo ships, 'dodge ships'- as it was known growing up, trying to smuggle into Europe with many dying along the journey? Why are the youths of our continent camping on the seashores of Morocco and Libya trying to sail their way into Europe? Why is it that almost every African in Africa today is trying to travel to the western world? The story is no longer about who did what to us but rather what we are doing to ourselves.

"Bury me in the ocean, with my ancestors that jumped from the ships, because they knew death was better than bondage"
—KILLMONGER-BLACK PANTHER MOVIE CHARACTER.

One thing the history books have in common is that my ancestors did everything within their powers to avoid the journey across the Atlantic Ocean. Some of them took their own lives, committing suicide by jumping off slave ships into bottomless oceans. They fought their captors with all the might they had. Today, my generation is willing to sacrifice almost everything in order to escape the horrors of the place we call HOME just to become 'second-class' citizens in the West. What are we running away from? Pan-African leaders are preaching Pan-Africanism while their (our) children are all western citizens. We have convinced ourselves with lies that *"Mama Africa is beautiful"*, yet man   ""
leave Africa for the poorest western country in
with no remorse. Who are we fooling?

Don't get me wrong; I am not shaming Africans for coming or wanting to travel the world. My Lord is my witness I am not faulting or trying to shame our continent. Who wouldn't want to see the world to appreciate God's creation? My high school economics class taught me that the first step towards solving problems is recognizing and defining them. I am not finger pointing, neither am I suggesting a silver-bullet solution to our problems. I am only looking at myself in the mirror and seeing our continent for what it is and nothing more.

For anyone to comprehend why Africans are deserting and abandoning the land we all claim to love so dearly we must first understand what we are running away from.

Chapter One

Chapter Two

Our Nightmares:

"*Africa, we are co-authors of our own misfortune*"
—PLO LUMUMBA

Africa is a continent full of promises and contradictions. It is blessed with over one billion people with the population projected to reach two billion by 2050. It is endowed with a big human capital. It is one of the richest (if not the richest) continent in term of natural resources. And yet it remains to be the laughing stock of the rest of the world. We contribute less than two percent in world industrial production. We create rich economies with poor populations like in the case of Nigeria and South Africa (the two largest economies in Africa). The atmosphere is filled with wars and rumors of war at every corner of the continent, and the young people are fleeing our continent. In this chapter, I will delve into some of Africa's contradictions that are forcing our people on an exodus and weakening our independent nations.

I. Wars: Conflicts

According to the International Displacement Monitoring Center (IDMC), there are more than nine million displaced refugees due to internal conflicts and wars in Africa. These are not the kinds of wars the world is familiar with. Normally soldiers fight wars and protect the lives and properties of the civilians. A soldier loves his/her country and protects its citizens. Wars have treaties and conflict resolution mechanisms. Soldiers kill enemies on the battlefield, but they do not prey on the innocent. Wars claim casualties during engagements. However, these are not the kind of wars we have been experiencing in Africa. What Africa has been experiencing is nothing short of pure EVIL and CRUELTY motivated by greed, selfishness, corruption, tribalism, religious cultism, political aggression, bad leadership, and downright ignorance. We take away books and pencils from the hands of our children and trade them for guns and bullets. We take them out of classrooms and force them into becoming child soldiers. We steal their innocence and turn them into killing machines. We rape our women and kill children.

The Liberian Civil War:

The first crime committed here is calling a war *"civil"*. I am officially changing the name to the *"Liberian Uncivil Cannibalism"*. Liberia, Africa's oldest democracy after gaining her independence from America (July 26, 1847), became known to the rest of the world in the early 1990's for its bloody civil war that left over 200,000 people dead and a third of its population displaced. The war lasted for 14 years. Liberians committed one of the most heinous crimes against their own citizens. I cannot think of any form of devilish demon that can overcome a person or hypnotize him/her into drinking the blood of their fellow human beings and eat their raw body flesh and heart out. The rebel groups claimed human blood and flesh make them invincible and stronger. I am still haunted by those images and sound bites from various documentaries. They did not only kill people, but they also drank their blood and feasted on their flesh. While the military and rebel groups engaged in the fights were predominantly fought by men, women and children were the largest victims. Women and children were often assaulted, raped, abducted, and murdered by these rebel groups. Liberian women had to witness their teenage sons get recruited into rebel groups, get drugged, and came back to inflict pain on their own people. They had to watch their daughters abducted as domestic slaves by day and sex slaves by night. They had to bear the pain of watching their husbands executed in the most dehumanizing manners by rebel groups. As a man with strong faith, I may not be able to give you any scientific proof that God exist outside of faith, but I can prove to you without doubt that there is a *"Devil"* and he existed in Liberia during those horrifying months and years.

The International Criminal Court (ICC), put to trial one of the men, Charles Taylor, who was partly responsible for these crimes, for his involvement with the Sierra Leonean 'un-civil' war and not for his crimes against Liberia and its people. Accepting the same Charles Taylor to rule over them is the debt the Liberians had to pay for peace. The Liberian women say it best, *"He killed my ma, he killed my pa, but I will vote for him"*. Voting for the same man who was responsible for the murders of their loved ones was the price they had to pay for peace and to save their own lives during their 1997 presidential elections.

"We believe as custodians of this society, tomorrow our children will ask us, Mama, what was your role during the crisis?"
—LEYMAH GBOWEE.

As disheartened as I am about man's inhumane actions towards his fellow man, I am equally impressed and encouraged by the humanity of the Liberian women for rising from the ashes of hate and evil meted out to them by their own children to standing up for peace and love. Prominent Liberian women such as Leymah Gbowee played very significant roles in the negotiation and peaceful reconciliation during the civil war and still continue to play significant roles in the rebuilding of Liberia. Liberia will go on to elect Africa's first woman president, Ellen Johnson Sirleaf, in 2006.

Rwandan Genocides:

Eighty-five percent of the Rwandan populations were from the Hutu tribe and 15% from the Tutsi, Twa, and Pygmy tribes. During Rwanda's colonial period, the Belgian colonial rulers favored the minority Tutsi tribe over the Hutus. Many Hutus saw this action as a tendency for the few to oppress the many, creating a legacy of tension that exploded into violence even before Rwanda gained its independence. The history of Tutsis and Hutus targeting and massacring each other has been going on for years before Burundi and Rwanda gained their independence from Belgium. In 1972 the world witnessed almost 300,000 Hutus murdered by a minority military government of mainly Tutsis in Burundi. A civil war broke out in Burundi, in 1993, after their first multi-party election that lasted up till 2005, with an estimated death toll of 300,000. As of this writing, the Hutus and Tutsis are still engaged in tribal conflicts in parts of Congo, Uganda, and Burundi. But nothing prepares the world for the 1996 bloody April massacre in Rwanda. The genocide began after a plane carrying respective Presidents of Rwanda and Burundi (Habyarimana and Cyprien Ntaryamira) was shot down, over the Rwandan capital Kigali, leaving no survivors. The Hutu extremists blamed the attack on the Tutsi rebels and so it began; the mass killings quickly spread from Kigali to the rest of the country.

To look at your own countrymen in their eyes, claim that they are not worthy of your bullets, and instead should face the most brutal form of death. You take a machete and cut them into pieces just because their national identification card reads Tutsi instead of Hutu is beyond human comprehension. To have the audacity to conveniently convince yourself that you were not killing humans, but cockroaches is sinful and satanic. Just like in the case of Yugoslavia, and many other genocides committed around the world, the international community's response, or lack thereof, came almost too late. The former Secretary General of the UN, Boutros Boutros-Ghali said, and I quote, *"The failure of Rwanda is 10 times greater than the failure of Yugoslavia. Because in Yugoslavia the international community was interested, was involved. In Rwanda nobody was interested"*, and 800,000 innocent men and women (including children) were massacred within 90 days just because they came from a different tribe. Over 2 million people, majority Hutus, became displaced in refugee camps across Zaire (present day Democratic Republic of Congo) and other neighboring countries. These killings were deliberate and executed with passion and hatred. This was arguably the most senseless war in Africa's history, not saying that any of them ever made sense.

Rwanda was able to forge a reconciliation government after the Genocide, with Pasteur Bizimungu, a Hutu, as President and Paul Kagame, a Tutsi, as vice president and minister of defense. In 2003 they adopted a new constitution and removed all references to ethnicity. More than twenty years later, the victims now live with the killers of their loved ones as neighbors. One can imagine this must be a very painful experience, but it is a sacrifice that is necessary for peace. Perpetrators faced their victims, confessed their crimes, and apologized for their actions. The former Rwandan Justice Minister, Tharcisse, described the reconciliation process as *"justice for all"*. Whether an apology constitutes justice for the victims is debatable, but it is a good start for a way forward. Once more women took the lead to shake the hands of the killers of their husbands, children, and loved ones as they forgive them, but forget they shall never do. Justice or no justice, Rwanda and Africa should never forget *"Bloody April"*. Today, the Rwandan economy continues to strive and its people enjoying relative peace under the leadership of President Kagame and that is a cause for optimism regarding the future of the continent.

The Somali 'Confusing' Chaotic Wars:

Majority of African wars, if not all, are senseless in my opinion, but the Somali war is just about the most confusing civil war in African history. It has so many different characters and armed groups, which made it so difficult to distinguish who was on which side and the purpose of their involvement in the war. Tribal warlords, religious warlords, rebel groups, criminal pirates, terrorist groups, famine, drought; think of any man-made human catastrophe and it existed in Somalia.

Somalia, known as the horn of Africa due to its protruding geographical location on the map of the continent, has its capital city as Mogadishu. Somalia gained independence on July 1st, 1960, after the amalgamation of British Somaliland and the Italian Somaliland as one state. Somalia is a perfect example of the residual effects of colonialism and the tragic blunder the colonial rulers left behind in Africa. Since attaining their independence, Somalia's growth has been very slow. Its international relations with its neighboring countries, Kenya, Ethiopia, and Djibouti, quickly deteriorated when their president, Mohamed Siad Barre, began *"land grabbing"* neighboring countries' territories and claimed that they belonged to Somalia.

In 1991, President Mohamed Siad Barre's government was overthrown by opposing clans and tribal warlords. The different tribes and clans failed to agree on which tribe their new leader should come from and the roles of each tribe in their new state. Their differences led Somalia to be disintegrated into multiple poorly defined tribal territories and settlements, Puntland, Somaliland, Jubaland, Rahanweyn land, Marihanland, and so on. Due to the tribal wars and lack of unity/concessions among the tribes, Somalia went on for two decades without a parliament or an organized system of government. Attempts from various international humanitarian missions to bring about reconciliation were noticeable and seemingly ongoing. However, the 1993 *"Black Hawk Down"* incident, which left 18 American soldiers on a peace mission dead after their chopper was gunned down, swayed the international community away from Somalia. From that point on Somalia became a quagmire of terror and horror.

The Somali civil war went through different phases since the fall of President Barre. From 1991 to 2000, Somalia has been devastated by tribal and ethnic conflicts, famine, drought, and lack of international intervention that left almost half a million people dead and many more displaced, according to the Necrometrics (20th century death tolls). Post September 11, 2001 also showed the emergence of religious terror groups in Somalia, such as Al-Shabaab, who extended their terror campaign into neighboring countries such as Kenya. This caught the attention of the international organizations, which will later motivate the African Union (AU) to put its act together and send humanitarian military help to Somalia. The long-lasting absence of law and order in Somalia bred new players in the Somali conflict. In 2011, the world witnessed the rise of Somali pirates; they hijacked ships passing through the Somali waters, thus becoming a major threat to international trade. In 2011 Somalia experienced the worst drought in 6 decades since independence, which left millions of people on the verge of starvation and led to a massive exodus of Somalis to neighboring countries.

All these events finally forced the AU, to set up a peace-keeping force called African Union Mission to Somalia (AMISOM) and deployed to Somalia to help restore order. AMISOM was made up of Military task forces from African countries such as Uganda, Burundi, Kenya, Nigeria, and Sierra Leone. They succeeded in pushing Al-Shabaab out of Southern Somali towns they once controlled. On May 9th, 2013, the Deputy Secretary General of the UN, Jan Eliasson, reported that AMISOM task force incurred over 3000 casualties in the Somali war. Due to the tremendous sacrifice and heroism of these soldiers, Somalia is currently relatively stable, although the threats of Al-Shabaab still exist. AMISOM task forces were scheduled to remain in Somalia until the end of 2016. But in July of 2018 the AMISOM mandate had been extended until May of 2019. With the constant imminent threat of terror organization in the sub region, it is more likely that that mandate may be extended once again.

Somalia, which is another tragic story of Africa, where our young men pick up arms against each other and destroy lives, also proves that there is strength in Unity. The AU and AMISOM have proven that Africans are capable of resolving their own issues without foreign or western assistance or interventions. For that reason, I am hopeful for the future leaders of our continent.

Sierra Leone, 'Cry Freetown':

Diamonds last forever but at what cost? More than 70% of Sierra Leoneans have never seen a diamond in their lives. Majority of the victims of *"Cry Freetown"* don't even know why they were killed or the worth of a Diamond. One of the world's largest diamond was found in *"Salone"*, but little did Sierra Leoneans know it was going to cost them arms and legs, literally. The Sierra Leone Civil war began on the 23rd of March 1991, when the Revolutionary United Front (RUF), with the support of Liberian forces under the leadership of Charles Taylor (NPFL), attempted to overthrow President Joseph Momoh's government. This triggered an eleven-year civil war the continent has never encountered. The war lasted between 1991 and 2002, it left more than 50,000 people dead and over 2 million people displaced as refugees in neighboring countries and beyond.

People were not only killed but family members were made to watch these killings. The RUF militias raped mothers and forced their husbands and children to participate in the acts. They drugged children and force them to kill their own siblings and parents. The killing and caricature of the victims was unimaginable but chopping of people's limbs and allowing them to relive the horrors over and over again is overbearing. How can anyone reason with a rebel group who pledged to *"Operation no living Soul"*? They kill anyone and everyone without discrimination. I had promised myself that I wouldn't cry (watching Cry Freetown: the documentary) because I am 'no cry baby'. However, I couldn't help but imagine the disgust of having to choose between killing my mother or be killed. No child deserves to go through such horrific experiences and dilemma.

The UN forces raided rebel-held areas and disarmed rebel groups. In January of 2002, the Sierra Leone civil war was declared over. This war though was not supposed to have started in the first place. Sierra Leone was supposed to be the beacon and shining light of West Africa; it has all the ingredients and natural resources to become an economically independent nation post-independence. It has West Africa's first national university, the Fourah Bay College. The land is endowed with natural resources, which instead turned out to become a curse for its people. Today Sierra Leone continues to be devastated with socio-economic crisis. The recent Ebola outbreak that left over 3000 people dead and millions of dollars spent almost brought the nation's economy crumbling.

Sudan (North and South), Darfur (Western):

Since gaining their independence in 1956 from their colonial rulers, Britain, Sudan has been involved in two civil wars that left over 2 million people dead and over 4 million displaced. The humanitarian situation, especially in South Sudan, got so bad that International Humanitarian Organizations described it as a *"lost generation who lacks educational opportunities, access to basic healthcare, and basic human needs such as food and shelter"*. Many experts reported that the root cause of the Sudanese crisis was due to competition for scarce resources between Arab-speaking and non-Arab-speaking Sudanese.

Human rights groups accused both North and South Sudan for enlisting child soldiers in their militant groups. This seems to be a very common practice during conflicts in Africa. On March 4, 2009, the ICC issued an arrest warrant for the Sudanese President Omar Al Bashir for his crimes against humanity and in July of 2010, other allegations, such as genocide, were added on his charge sheet, which should have technically made him a prisoner in his own country. The warrant for his arrest is yet to be honored by countries (e.g. South Africa, Kenya, and Saudi Arabia) he has visited since the issuance of the arrest warrant.

Sudan, located in Northeastern Africa, was the third largest country in the continent prior to its subdivision into north and south countries. With the exception of South Africa's apartheid (which ended), no other country in Africa is as divided based on ethnicity and skin color as Sudan. Sudan has a population of 22 million people that are divided into two distinct cultures, Arabs and Blacks, with the majority speaking Arabic. The nation that was known as Sudan was divided into two parts, North and South Sudan. The modern-day South Sudan gained its independence from Sudan in July of 2011 and has a population of 6 million people.

In South Sudan, oil reserves were first discovered in a region call Unity State, in 1970. Ironically, Unity State happened to be one of the poorest and divided states in South Sudan. The international oil companies that engage in oil exploration contributed to the massive displacement of the indigenous people. Rival militant groups threw babies into wildfires when their parents refused to evacuate the oil station areas. The entire South Sudanese nation only controls about 5% of the oil production they sell to the world market. China controls 40% of the oil development activities while Malaysia and India each have 30 and 25 percent stakes in the oil industry respectively. History has proven that the Asians were not involved in colonizing or enslaving Africans, but is this not equivalent or worse than modern day slavery and colonialism? I am not even sure if I should blame them for this is a very common practice in third world countries endowed with natural resources. They don't even hire Sudanese people to work on their own oil fields; they import workers from . . . yep you guessed right, China, India, and Malaysia. But the Sudanese are getting killed and starved to death just because they happened to be born on the wrong land that has useful natural resources. As a member of the United Nations Security Council, China has been accused of blocking many UN resolution bills regarding the

Sudan crisis in an attempt to appease the Sudanese government. Coincidentally (or not), Sudan is China's largest oil provider. For only 5% of an Oil revenue, which less than 5% of the population enjoys, the fighters almost wiped out 95% of the supposed-to-be real benefactors. I don't know if this is *"greed"* or just pure *"evil"*. Meanwhile, the current president of South Sudan, Salva Kiir Mayardit, and his son, Munuti Salva Kiir, who called himself the "*Donald Trump of Africa*" are living a very lavish lifestyle.

While Southern and Northern Sudan went their separate ways, not many people took into consideration how that may affect Western Sudan, Darfur. Darfur remains to be underdeveloped and marginalized. Many experts describe it as a *"ticking timing bomb"* that can explode anytime. Villages in Darfur are no strangers to air strike bombings from Sudanese Air Forces. Air strikes are usually followed up with guerilla groups, the Janjaweed, who kill anyone they can find, rape women and children, and loot properties. Just like South Sudan, Western Sudan, Darfur, is also requesting for independence from Sudan, and Sudan is reluctant to consider that as an option. More recently, Sudan has been fighting conflicts in Blue Nile and South Kordofan states as well.

Sometimes it makes me wonder whether the lack of meaningful natural resource in my home country, The Gambia, is a blessing after all.

In February of 2019, amid antigovernment protests in Sudan, Omar Al Bashir declared a yearlong state of emergency. On April 11th, 2019, the Sudanese political turmoil took another turn, the Sudanese military carried out a very shady takeover against President Omar Al-Bashir's 30-year dictatorial regime. They claimed to have placed Al-Bashir and some of his top aides in a house arrest. His former defense minister Ibn Auf appointed himself as the new interim leader overseeing a two-year transitional period. Upon intense protest, just a day later he resigned, and another military general Burhan took over. Burhan is believed to be more credible and popular among the rank-and-file of the military soldiers. But the Sudanese civil society groups and political parties are still not convinced, and they are demanding for a complete transition from military to civilian rule with immediate effect.

International observers are closely monitoring and cautiously welcoming the regime change in Sudan. From past experiences, as in the Cases of Egypt and Libya, the ousting of dictatorial regimes birthed new special interest criminal and rebel organizations. The political dilemma that the international community is faced with now is whether the fall of Al-Bashir regime is going to lead to the rise of the Sudan Islamist Movement, which is believed to have very close ties with the Muslim Brotherhood, an organized terrorist movement in the region.

On the same day, April 11, 2019, coincidentally, just few hours after the military takeover in Sudan that ended Al-Bashir regime, Pope Francis made a dramatic call to the South Sudanese political leaders at the Vatican in Rome begging them to *"stay in peace"*. The timing of these event as mentioned is supposedly completely coincidental. The South Sudanese leaders' spiritual retreat at the Vatican was scheduled to take place without any prior knowledge of the Sudan military takeover. There, the Pope made a symbolic gesture by kneeling down and kissing the feet of President Salva Kiir, and opposition political leader, Riek Machar. It was one of the most humbling and genuine gestures I have

Chapter Two

seen displayed by a global icon in my life time. All previous attempts to bring peace to South Sudan have failed causing over 400, 000 deaths since 2013. Now the world awaits to see if the efforts of one of the most influential spiritual leaders in the world will have a breakthrough in establishing everlasting peace in South Sudan.

The once third largest country in Africa now divided into two nations, as of this publication; both South Sudan and Sudan are in turmoil and political crisis. And the main losers are the ordinary civilians. Without proper diplomatic interference, both (Northern) Sudan and South Sudan could potentially go into flames.

Guinea Bissau Coup D'états:

With cashew nuts as its primary source of foreign exchange, the formerly Portuguese Guinea, Guinea Bissau was considered one of the potential models for African development. Guinea Bissau had the potential to create a respectable economy based on the production of cash crops. Unfortunately, after a long arm struggle for independence the country is now one of the poorest in the world.

This country probably has the most tragic democracy in the history of Africa. This is the only country that never had a democratically elected president complete his/her presidential term since independence (1975). They are either killed or overthrown by imbeciles in uniform who called themselves soldiers. Any fool who owns a gun and a couple of buddies think they can become a president. By the way this seems to be the case for many African countries. This country manifests the true ignorance and lack of democracy in the continent. You don't even have to be a citizen of that country to become an illegitimate president. Just be a good killer or murderer and seek funding for weapons from drug lords in exchange for pushing a few of their merchandise across the continent. Guinea Bissau is a major drug hub for cocaine smuggling from Latin America to Europe. The drug lords seem to always have a huge interest in the local politics of the country. The fact that they never had an elected president complete a presidential term alone says a lot. The Latin American Mafias and corrupt local military men determine presidential term limits in Guinea Bissau. The more you corporate with them the longer your presidential term limit.

In 2014, their new president, Jose Mario Vaz, won the presidential elections and maintain relative stability warranting the EU naming it the most improved country in the Global Peace Index ranking in 2015. But after a major dispute between the president and his Prime Minister resulting to his sacking later that same year, the country took a major step back into another political turmoil.

It is important to note that coup d'états are not peculiar to Guinea Bissau. Africa has witnessed at least 200 successful and failed coup attempts. The first military coup d'état in Africa took place in Togo only a year after their independence. And the last military coup as of this writing took place in Sudan, 2019. Since independence 40 out of 54 African countries had experienced military coup d'états. Nigeria, Africa's largest economy and population, had 8 coup attempts between 1966 and 1999. Burkina Faso had 10, Burundi 6, Chad 6, Ghana 6, Comoros 6, Mauritania 6, Sudan 7, Ethiopia 5, Libya 5, Sierra Leone 5, Central African Republic 5, and Benin 5, just to name a few. The end results for all military coups are the same. Poor economic growth, high inflation, abuse of human rights, high poverty rate, high corruption rate, breeding of dictators, and in worst cases wars and conflicts. The financial losses associated with military coups in Africa cannot be quantified. And Africa unceremoniously lost some of its great leaders and scholars such as Kwame Nkrumah and Patrice Lumumba, Ken Saro-Wiwa via military coups, which I will buttress on in subsequent chapters.

Democratic Republic of Congo:

Congo is home to one of the most patriotic and loyal sons of Africa, Patrice Lumumba. Congo gained its independence from Belgium on the 30th of June 1960. On the 17th of January 1961, Patrice Lumumba was executed by Belgian-led Katangese troops. Since they shed the blood of a man who millions regarded as a true African son on Congolese soil, Congo has not seen absolute peace since. Sometimes I wonder if they are cursed by Lumumba's death. Congo depicts the perfect picture of the contradiction that plagues the African continent. Congo is the richest country on earth in terms of natural resources and yet one of the poorest countries in terms of Gross Domestic Product (GDP).

As if the notorious genocidal regime of the Belgian colonial government against the Congolese was not enough. A civil war broke out in 1996 that brought an end to President Mobutu's 31-year rule and left the country destabilized. The war included 9 African countries (Angola, Namibia, Zimbabwe, Uganda, Rwanda, Burundi, Tanzania, Sudan, and Congo itself), and comprised of twenty-two local armed rebel groups, and multiple UN peacekeeping forces. The war is known as Africa's world war.

During that time period, I think this country should have been called the *"Undemocratic Republic of Congo"*. Eighty percent of the world's resources used in the manufacturing of cell phones and other smart devices come from Congo. The mineral wealth of the country is estimated to be over 24 trillion dollars. Because of these economic gains, Belgium, Angola, Namibia, Zimbabwe, Uganda, Rwanda, Burundi, Tanzania, Sudan, and the Congolese themselves refused to allow peace in that land. Think of any form of precious stone you can imagine, and you will most likely find it in Congo. The prize for such wonderful blessing from Mother Nature is 5.4 million deaths and still counting. The sounds of gunfire are music to the ears. The only constant source of employment is jumping from one rebel group to a more lucrative rebel group. One of the richest men in Africa and in the world, Jean-Pierre Bemba, was the leader of the most organized rebel group in Congo before he was sent to jail by the ICC for his involvement in the Congo war. A Congolese billionaire, out of all the great things he could have done for his people chose from *"the goodness of his heart"* to fund a rebel group. Congo experienced the deadliest war since World War II, but it still manages to be the most silent and least talked about war. The man responsible for some of those killings, Jean-Pierre Bemba, was at some point rewarded with a vice-presidency position as part of a peace treaty between the rebel groups and the government.

Katharine Viner, a very famous blogger describes Eastern Congo as *"the rape capital of the world and the worst place on earth to be a woman"*. More than half of the women of Congo have either been raped or sexually exploited since 1998. Rape and the exploitation of women continue to be a growing concern in Congo. Former child soldiers who were trained to do one thing and one thing only; to take human life mercilessly, are left wondering around with no rehabilitation or training to assimilate back into civilized society. These children will become adults and future custodians of the Congolese society with very little moral empathy or love in their hearts. They are victims of a society that turned them into 'wasted generations.'

From Liberia to Sierra Leone, Congo to Burundi, Somalia to Guinea Bissau, our continent has turned the future custodians of our societies into menaces to the very societies they are supposed to protect someday.

The former Congolese president, Joseph Kabila, passed a bill to keep him in power past his two-term constitutional mandate. This has given rise to more political tensions in Congo. Civil rights groups, religious leaders, and other influential groups have spoken against this action, but the president ignored their calls. He eventually succumbed to public and international outcry and decided to step down. Congo has elected a new president and a new republic is on the horizon. The children of Patrice Lumumba are given another opportunity to get their acts together, but some experts argue that Congo may never experience complete peace because of the multiple interest groups fighting for its resources, but I remain hopeful.

Our continent is infested with crimes of demonization and humiliation. There are many other wars that warrant equal scrutiny such as the Central African Republic war, the war in Egypt, the Ethiopia-Eritrea war, the Ugandan war, the Mozambique war, the Nigeria Biafra war, the Mali Tuareg rebellion, the Burundi war, and so many other wars. But I am convinced that I have presented enough evidence in this literature to make my point. We have all fallen short of the glory of God and that of mankind and have sinned against our continent. We can all do a thing or two more than we have done for our continent. Killing and feasting on the flesh of our own kind, overthrowing our democratically elected governments, chopping off the limbs of our own siblings, chopping our own children into pieces, witch-hunting and jailing our *"political enemies"*, and raping our women are all self-inflicted. Fixing it will become a collective responsibility for all people who benefited from Africa and its resources including the western world. But Africa must take the lead.

Speaking of the West, Africans need to learn that the West are not going to save us. Help is not on the way. We look sad and pathetic on international news channels begging for Western countries and the UN to come and rescue us. Bill Clinton said in 1994 during the Rwandan Genocide, *"The US will not send military aid to nations we don't have interest in"*. There has to be some sort of political gain on the side of the West in order for them to sacrifice their sons and daughters in an attempt to rescue us. The best thing the West may offer us may be to pressure our leaders to convict our so-called war lords in tribunals.

Tribunals such as the ICC are trying, but when it comes to saving human lives by preventing recurrence, trying is not enough. They often leave the big criminals and go after the small criminals. In the cases where they convict the big criminals, they usually charge them with lesser crimes. It is like charging and convicting an international heroine dealer for smuggling tobacco. In very rare situations where the big criminals are convicted for their big crimes, their jail conditions are treated as vacations. Convicting someone for being responsible for the killings of hundreds/thousands/

millions of people either directly or indirectly sounds very *noble*, if the consequence is putting them in a free housing, call it jail if you want, with free meals, free healthcare, free books to read, free gym to workout in whenever they feel like, then there is something fundamentally wrong with both our legal and moral conscience. I consider that an *extended vacation*. This is a vacation paid for by the same people they victimized. Call me a conservative if you think I sound like one but there is something wrong with this picture. I have a very strong feeling that if we gave the innocent babies from Liberia, the babies who had their hearts ripped out of their chest and consumed by their murderers the option to go to the tribunal or endure the pain they experienced, I think they will choose the former. I may be wrong, but I doubt it.

There are many other issues that contribute to the self-exodus of Africans from Africa and hinder our progress since independence. Disease, poverty, low political IQ, illiteracy, natural disasters, poor social conditions, economic reasons, poor leadership, and so on, but all of these issues can be overcome if we can first secure PEACE.

II. Poor Leadership:

"Africa's biggest problem today lies with the leadership. They are so removed from the people that they are looked upon as foreigners. They are driven by self-interest, so excessive that their people's interests are forgotten, hardly different from the colonial masters"
—JOHN HAYFORD

When the colonial governors left Africa post-independence, they left us with their nice gubernatorial mansions they used to live in, they left behind their nice cars they used to drive, they left some of their nice clothes they used to wear, they left their administrative books and policies they used to police and colonize us with, they left us the schools their children used to attend, they left their African security personnel who were protecting colonial interest, and off they went. We danced and celebrated to the tune of independence.

Free at last, we are finally Independent we claimed. We replaced the white colonial masters with black African rulers. Our new masters moved into the nice mansions vacated by the white masters, they wore the clothes left behind by the colonial rulers, they drove their nice cars, they sent their kids to the schools the former colonial masters' kids attended, they used their policies and administrative books and draft constitutions for us, and used the same black African security men the colonial masters used to protect their colonial interest. They became our heads of state and collected taxes from us just like our colonial masters did. I therefore submit the question to you, are we truly independent? Are these the type of leadership free people should have? Or did we just replace white colonialism with a new era of *"domestic servitude"* by our own black masters? Our colonial masters left us poor and disorganized and we are still poor and disorganized post-independence. I think our independence anniversaries should only be a moment for us to reexamine our independence and see how far we've come and assess whether we got rid of colonialism and the colonial masters in the early 1960's for good or whether we just replaced them with black faces commonly known as our presidents.

These are not over exaggerations on my part. While I acknowledge individuals like Paul Kagame of Rwanda, late Nelson Mandela of South Africa, John Magufuli of Tanzania, Danny Faure of Seychelles, Ameenah Gurib of Mauritius, Ian Khama of Botswana, and Ellen Johnson Sirleaf of Liberia for their exemplary leadership, majority of African leaders leave a very bad legacy following their tenure. Swaziland has one of the world's highest HIV prevalence rate (at 35 percent) and the lowest life expectancy at shocking 33 years, under the leadership of King Mswati III. President Omar Al- Bashir of Sudan's reign has been characterized by wars which consumed over one million casualties throughout his 30-year leadership. Unbeknownst to him however, he too was soon to be victim of a presidential takeover. During President Mugabe's leadership in Zimbabwe, the country had the highest unemployment rate in the world, over 60 percent. President Jose Eduardo dos Santos of Angola runs the country like his own personal investment portfolio. His daughter is the wealthiest woman in Angola and his cousin is his Vice President. Despite of all the natural resources (diamonds) the country is blessed with, 68 percent of Angolans lives under the international poverty line. President Teodoro Obiang Nguema Mbasogo of Equatorial Guinea is Africa's longest serving president. Despite the fact that the country has one of the highest per capita income in the world, majority of Equatoguineans don't have access to clean drinking water, one of the worst child mortality rates (20% of children under five dies), and one of the worst human rights records in the world. And for good measures, his first son is his Vice President and in line to succeed him.

Many of our leaders promised us the heavens and swear by their Gods that Africa is the best continent on earth when they themselves have no faith in our continent. We have public schools, but they send their children to private schools with western curriculums, because they have no faith in our local teachers and schools. We have public hospitals, but they send their sick loved ones to private hospitals and sometimes abroad because they have no faith in our local doctors. We have local food producers/farmers, but they conduct their grocery shopping in foreign-brand supermarkets. We have our local engineers and constructors, but they import foreign Engineers to construct our roads and buildings because they have no faith in our engineers. We have books written by our people with Doctorate degrees, but they prefer to read books written by foreign authors. We have our local fashion designers, but they only take pride in foreign-tailored brands. We have our own local entertainers and artists, but they find more joy in foreign entertainers. When our citizens cry for help our governments don't listen unless we consult foreign organizations/countries to intervene on our behalf before they take our plight seriously. While many of our leaders are no different from the colonial masters, they seem completely oblivious to the realities of our continent.

III. Dictators

"Dictators free themselves but they enslave the people"
—Charlie Chaplin

Soldiers defend nations, but African Soldiers for the most part choose to defend individuals. They defend individuals who treat their own people worse than the slave masters treated our ancestors. They claim to own everything that belongs to their people, they take away their human dignity and often claim to be holy men sent to rescue their people. They live above the law and in most cases are the law themselves. Dictators and bad leaders are worse than wars because they watch their people die slow deaths and pretend like they are the best things that ever happen to mankind since 'Jollof rice'. They often engage in self-aggrandizement, self-proclamation, and self-entitlement with gravy titles. They bestow upon themselves phony academic, military, and other noble accolades they can never achieve with their academic and professional integrity alone . . . King of Kings, President for Life, The Redeemer, The Conqueror, The Seer, The Savior, The Teacher, The Man of . . . you fill in the blank. One example is former president of The Gambia whose full name before becoming a president was Yahya Jammeh, by the time he was out of office, his full name read as "His Excellency retired Colonel Sheikh Professor Alhaji Dr. Yahya Abdul-Aziz Awal Jemus Junkung Jammeh Nasirudeen Babili Mansa".

These types of leaders! their actions are not out of mistakes; they are very well calculated and deliberate. They preach democracy but silence anyone who dares to defend the same democracy that they preach. Dare challenge them and you see the wrath of what they can do to you and yours. They handicap the structure of governance during their kingship thus making the post dictatorship eras even worse. African countries with dictatorial regimes can never win. If you let them rule, they keep their people in bondage for eternity. If you challenge them, they slaughter their entire population in the name of *"love for country"*. If the people's prayers are ever to be answered by the Gods of our ancestors and change happens for whatsoever reason, they leave their nations in chaos and total anarchy. Choose your poison or should I say lesser evil. Africa has bred some of the worst dictators in human history and still does. Paul Biya of Cameroon, Robert Mugabe of Zimbabwe, Siad Barre of Somalia, Omar Al-Bashir of Sudan, Hissene Habre of Chad, Idi Amin Dada of Uganda, and Yahya Jammeh of The Gambia; just to name a few. It is not possible to develop a badly governed country, and African dictators have been making sure that this is the case in many African countries since their respective independence.

IV. Lost Pride and Dignity

"If you make a man feel that he is inferior, you do not have to compel him to accept an inferior status, for he will seek it himself. If you make a man think that he is justly an outcast, you do not have to order him to the back door. He will without being told; and if there is no back door, his very nature will demand one."
—Carter G. Woodson,
the Miseducation of the Negro

Africa needs to demonstrate her maturity and seriousness as a continent. We are easily excited and quick to celebrate things that may not even be worthy of celebration. In April of 2019, the Malawi government posted on their official Facebook page that their Minister of Information and Communication Technology, Henry Mussa, officially received two motorbikes from Ambassador Liu Hongyang, of the people republic of China as donations. The minister proudly thanked the Chinese diplomat and posed for a picture with the two motorbikes. How embarrassing and desperate must one be for a whole state minister to attend such humiliation and to have the audacity to post it on the government official platform?

We are quick to count our chickens before they are ever hatched. Our ancestors were jumping for joy when the colonial master's ships first landed on the shores of Africa. And many years after independence, our children jump for joy and celebrate with the mere sightings of western tourists in our continent. President Obama's Global Entrepreneurship Summit in Africa was celebrated by Kenyans and Africans alike as though he was the second coming of Jehovah. The Kenyan streets were cleaned and decorated with American flags, homeless street children were rounded up and detained at police stations, the banks closed early, government offices were shut down, the Kenyans were encouraged to come out in their numbers to welcome him, which they did, and all their media houses (both print and digital) focused their attention on President Obama's visit. While I applaud President Obama for his remarkable and historic visit to Kenya and for being the first U.S president to visit the country, I am equally lost for words by the lack of self-esteem exercised by Kenyans and Africa. For a nation that is struggling to protect her citizens against Al-Shabaab terror attacks, Nairobi was arguably the safest and most secure city in the whole world at least for a couple of days during Obama's stay.

There is no price value one can attach to inspiring and motivating an entire country and continent for that matter. I am therefore very grateful for President Obama's visit. If nothing else, he placed the world's attention on Kenya and Africa at least for a couple of days. Obama came and did his best to articulate Africa's problems and the measures the continent needs to take to remedy them. Just like he did back in 2009, when he visited Ghana and was quoted as saying *"Africa don't need strong men, it needs strong institutions."* He brought with him investors with great entrepreneurship opportunities. We cheered and clapped for every word that left his lips. And just like in 2009, Obama is back in the U.S.A again addressing U.S issues (as a former president). Back in Africa, many leaders such as Teodoro Obiang Nguema of Equatorial Guinea, Paul Biya of Cameroon, Denis Sassou of Congo, Yoweri Museveni of Uganda, et al are still holding on to power and refusing to allow new political leaders to emerge. And each of these men have been in office for over 25 years. Rwanda's lower house of parliament voted to allow President Paul Kagame to extend his rule beyond a second term that ended in 2017 and possibly stay on until 2034 (reported by Reuters). Togo's parliament has voted a constitutional change allowing President Faure Gnassingbe, whose family has ruled Togo since 1967, to run two more terms and potentially remain in power until 2030 (reported by Punch). People in Burundi have voted for a new constitution that effectively paves the way for President Pierre Nkurunziza, who came into power in 2005, to serve until 2034 (reported by Buzz Feed News). And a constitutional court in Uganda has validated a constitutional amendment that removes an age limit for the country's leader, clearing the way for long-serving President Yoweri Museveni to remain in power for life. Our leaders are more focused on strengthening their grips on power instead of focusing on real issues that are detrimental to our continent. Corruption is still alive and vibrant, and poverty is more stricken today than before independence. Per the world economic forum, Somalia, South Sudan, Equatorial Guinea, Sudan, Burundi, Libya, Angola Chad, Congo, et al are among some of the most corrupt nations in the world. Our continent is still not experiencing breakthroughs in international trade, and foreign investors are only marginally investing in Africa. Africa contributes less than 2 percent in global industrial production.

Soon after President Obama's Kenya visit our excitement died down, the streets of Nairobi went back to being dirty, street children were released back into the streets, and Kenya became fragile and vulnerable again to terrorist attacks. The once united Kenya, hitherto for only few days, that stood together to welcome their *"son"* home, returned to their tribal and ethnic affiliations. Sometimes I wonder if even the second coming of Christ will be enough to give us sustainable enthusiasm and self-pride about our continent.

As president Kennedy once said, *"America does what is in the interest of America"*. I couldn't help but kept on thinking about these words throughout Obama's visit to Kenya. Was he there for the interest of both the U.S.A and Kenya/Africa or was he just doing what any U.S. president in his position would have done; doing *"what is in the interest of America"*? I pray and hope that it is the former. The truth is that not even the most powerful man on earth (at the time) can perform miracles for Africa. No amount of foreign importation of entrepreneurs and investors can rescue our continent for us. Africans must take the lead in our own renaissance. Things that are lacking in West Africa are being excessively produced in East Africa and vice-versa. Things that are lacking in the South are produced abundantly in the North and vice-versa. Yet African countries only conduct about 40% trade among themselves. Not even the Global Entrepreneurship Summit led by the most inspiring leader of our time can remedy that for us. If African economies are to blossom, Africans must start producing/manufacturing a lot more things we consume and trade among ourselves.

In 2002, most African countries entered into an Economic Partnership Agreement (EPA) negotiations with the European Union (EU). In other words, a favorable Raw Material Initiative trade was born in the interest of the EU. This agreement ensures that the EU will always have sufficient market access to Africa's raw materials at very reasonable prices. It seems like the continent has leased our independence back to the Europeans. In my opinion Africa do not have a supply problem, we have a distribution problem. We produce the things we don't need, export them, and import things we could be producing locally. We produce potatoes in Rwanda and Uganda and export them abroad, but we import potato chips and French fries. We produce coffee beans in Tanzania and Kenya and export them, but we import coffee. We produce cocoa in Cameroon and Nigeria and export them, but we import chocolate. We produce peanuts in The Gambia and Senegal and export them, but we import peanut butter. We produce oil in Sudan and Nigeria and export them, but we import petrol. We mine diamonds in Sierra Leone and Angola and export them, but we import jewelries. We add no value to the things we produce. We provide the rest of the world with all their raw material needs and leave Africa with nothing. Rice is one of the most staple food items in Africa, but we are content with importing it from Asia. Per the African Development Bank, Africa spends over 35 billion dollars annually importing food. How can a continent that cannot feed its population become economically independent? I am afraid the oxygen we breathe for free in Africa, we will one day export and buy it back once it is branded with a foreign label. As Ali Mazrui said, *"Africa produces what it does not consume and consumes what it does not produce"*. Africa is a continent with very low self-esteem.

The good news is that Africa still holds 30% of the world's reserves and over 60 different metals and minerals including diamonds, salt, gold, iron, cobalt, uranium, copper, bauxite, silver, petroleum, fresh water, and several agricultural products. If we get our acts together, we may still have a chance. Africa needs to start adding value to our local produce before we export them to the rest of the world. We must start branding our products and take pride in African creation. There is still hope but we need urgency and methodical precision in the decisions we make.

We need to build a continent where our children will know where we came from and why they are free. We must restore our African pride solely motivated by our dignity as Africans.

V. Poor Economic Integration Schemes:

In the early years of the 21st century, West African countries came up with a plagiarized scheme from the European Union to set up a single currency for ECOWAS member states. They set up an interim organization headquartered in Ghana in the year 2000; named it West Africa Monetary Institute (WAMI). This was going to become the future West African Bank. The European Monetary Institute (EMI) of the EU inspired it. Just like the EMI did for the EU, the WAMI also came up with an economic integration strategy to merge their currencies. They were going to start with none CFA Franc using countries and then slowly merge the rest of the Franco African states. Ten criteria were put in place, as a prerequisite for all the participating member countries to satisfy before this new currency, Eco Currency, was to be launched. There were four primary criteria and 6 secondary criteria.

The four primary criteria were:

- A single digit inflation rate at the end of each year.
- A fiscal deficit of no more than 4% of the GDP.
- A central bank deficit financing of no more than 10% of the previous year's tax revenues.
- Gross external reserves that can give import cover for a minimum of three months.

And the six secondary criteria were:

- Prohibition of new domestic default payments and liquidation of existing ones.
- Tax revenue should be equal to or greater than 20% of the GDP.
- Wage bill to tax revenue equal to or greater than 20%.
- Public investment to tax revenue equal to or greater than 20 percent.
- A stable real exchange rate.
- And a positive real interest rate.

Unfortunately, only Ghana was able to meet all criteria by the end of 2011. And by the end of 2012 not even a single member country meets all the criteria, including Ghana, per reports by the West African Monetary Zone (WAMZ). And after few years later, it seems more unrealistic today, especially after witnessing the Eurocurrency suffering tremendously. Africa, we are notorious *"monkey see, monkey do"* practitioners. We are always trying to meet other continents' standards instead of meeting our own standards. We always copy the rest of the world. And the biggest benefactor of innovation and creativity are their authors and creators. We will always be a step behind unless we can come up with innovative solutions targeting our unique problems. West African countries trade about only 10% among themselves, unlike the EU member states that had a huge inter-country trade within their member countries. Common sense dictates that we should first address our local issues such as inter-trade (free movement of goods and services), infrastructure, education, peace and stability, fiscal economic responsibility, and transparency within member countries as our priority. But instead, we jumped the necessary human and sub regional constraints that need to be looked at and drafted economic indicators with the expectation that poor member countries will miraculously resolve their individual problems by just sending them draft policies. Many observers wonder if it is possible that we can have a single currency in Africa. Yes, it can be done with the proper economic tools and measures put in place. Especially for a continent that is endowed with natural resources; we won't have to peg our currency against any foreign currency. We can peg our currency against the natural resources in our soil. That will be the first of its kind. We can industrialize our continent and start processing our resources instead of shipping them out in their raw form without adding any values to them. This will promote local inter-country trade and strengthen our currency in the process.

VI. Poverty and Unemployment:

One of the biggest issues Africa is confronted with is youth unemployment. The World Bank reported in 2011 that young people account for 60% of the unemployment rate in Africa. These numbers are in fact debatable if you take into account over 80% of the continent's workforce are either underemployed or working under very poor conditions. The same report added that up to 40% of young people who join rebel movements stated that they were motivated by lack of meaningful employment. These are some very worrisome statistics for the future of the continent. We have seen this to be true in northern Nigeria and parts of Cameroon where jobless youths are easily recruited by Boko Haram to join Islamic Extremist Movements. Per the Global Terrorism Database in 2015, Religious-inspired extremism has claimed the lives of more than 18,000 Africans and many of the actors of this horrendous acts are young people. And in 2017, the UN released a study, "Marginalization, perceived abuse of power pushing Africa's youth to extremism". Excerpts from the report stated that "the report is based on a two-year, in-depth study, including interviews with some 495 voluntary recruits who joined Africa's most prominent extremist groups, including Boko Haram and Al-Shabaab. According to UNDP estimates, some 33,300 people in Africa have lost their lives to violent extremist attacks between 2011 and early 2016."

African leaders met in Addis Ababa in 2009 where they discussed youth unemployment within the continent and feasible solutions to remedy it. They came out with a declaration to make the years between 2009 and 2018 *"African Youth Decade"*. In their declaration they stated that

"Creation of safe, decent, and competitive employment opportunities for young people" will be their main objective during the decade long declaration. The effectiveness of these policies drafted from this declaration to curb the youth unemployment rates are yet to be seen, and hence you forget it 2018 has come and retired. This seems to be the biggest dilemma of our continent since we gained our respective independence, our inability to create the necessary political and socio-economic framework to make use of the productivity of our youthful populations. Per my estimation based on population growth and distribution, over 27 million pupils graduate from high school every year in Africa. Out of that number only 4 million enroll into a university/college. That leaves a deficit of 23 million young people who graduate from high school every year with no skills or further education to be positive contributors in society. And in cases where we have university graduates, they are sometimes unemployable. Mohamed Yahya, a Regional Program Coordinator with United Nations Development Programme (UNDP) Africa, mentioned in his 2015 report, "A sidelined Youth: The soft underbelly of Africa rising", that there is an increasing mismatch between skilled employees offered and the level of quality workers demanded by the labor market. It seems like our educational systems and curriculums are often far behind the job market requirements, in essence they are producing unemployable graduates.

A serious progressive society ensures that they include young people and women in all sectors of their national development. This seems to be the contrary in many African societies. Young people are either marginalized or discouraged from playing any major role in their socio economics and political processes. This is largely due to societal norms, policies, and institutional constraints enacted by African states.

According to the 2014 CIA Factbook, almost 45% of Sub-Saharan Africa population live under the internationally recognized poverty line. Many critics argue that that number is very low due to the North African Arab nations who are included in the estimations. Tunisia had 4%, Morocco had 15 %, and Egypt and Algeria had 22 and 23% respectively. Chad and Liberia registering over 80% poverty rate individually. Out of the billion people living in the continent, over 218 million live in extreme poverty according to the Africa Rural Poverty report of 2009. Eastern and Southern Africa are considered places with the highest concentrations of poor people in the world. And over 70% of Africa's poor population live in Rural Africa. This history can be traced all the way back to the colonial systems. And since independence, African governments continue the culture of isolation of rural cities and villages in Africa, and increasingly government policies and investments in poverty reduction tend to favor urban over rural areas, just like the colonial days. This trend forces the mass exodus of rural inhabitants in search of greener pastures.

Despite the fact that almost half of the average African household expenditure goes towards food consumption, farming/agriculture in Africa is considered a poor man's profession and left in the hands of the old and fragile population. Ask any African to describe a farmer for you and they will describe a 65-year-old elderly man with torn clothes living in a tiny hut house in some remote village. The people with advance agricultural degrees and possessed modern farming techniques all choose life in big cities. They sit behind office desks and draft agricultural policies that affect the lives of everyday working farmers.

Our government policies and short-term thinking of our officials have only made agriculture unsustainable in Africa. African government policies are geared toward producing cash crops for export and fail to support farmers to produce enough food for local consumption. For Africa to attain self-sufficiency, it must feed its growing population. This will demand ingenuity and innovation to produce more food with fewer resources in more sustainable ways.

One famous American scientist, Abraham Maslow, came up with a hierarchy of needs for humans called the Maslow Pyramid. Food and security are on top of that pyramid. There is a certain order in things that determine the scale of preference of all advance societies. Before we can even look towards economic growth and independence, we must first endeavor for food security, and a stable, peaceful atmosphere without wars.

Chapter Three

Political Apathy:
The Silent Majority and Neutralism

"One of the penalties for refusing to participate in politics is that you end up being governed by your inferiors."

—PLATO

The saddest thing that happened to Africa post-independence is political apathy. The majority left the issue of politics and governance in the hands of a few. Africans treat our politicians and politics just as we treat Santa Claus and Christmas. We do not care about what they do, how they do it, when they do it, and who they do it for as long as they come around during election (Christmas) seasons bearing goodies (bribes) to lobby for our votes. Yet we complain bitterly when we do not like what they bring for us.

"The ultimate measure of a man is not where he stands in moments of comfort and convenience, but where he stands at the times of challenge and controversy"
—MARTIN LUTHER KING, JR.

Somewhere both within and outside the continent there's a silent majority of Africans hiding behind *"neutralism"* in regard to African politics. A majority that feels the pinch of their economy, and question their government's judicial and socio-economic policies, and want to see some positive changes in the way their Governments have been doing business since independence. The rich who are silent to safeguard and protect their status and wealth. The poor who are bought with money and gifts during political seasons. The illiterates who have little voter education and knowledge about their human and political rights. The opportunists who mainly follow their interests and will support anyone who serves their interest. And those who simply fear that not supporting the government will jeopardize their lives, their families, or their jobs and as a result opted to be silent. Unless more of us are willing to speak up and be heard now and beyond, so-called revolutionists and government propaganda will continue to hijack our national debates regarding the way forward, and the silent majority will become helpless and keep on getting caught up in cross fires between political rivals.

It seems like we Africans have gotten our hearts broken so many times that it doesn't even bother us anymore. Sometimes I even think we like it this way. Or perhaps our consciousness have been lulled into a coma and that we find more comfort in being sad than really doing anything about the things that make us sad. We are incompetent masters of nothingness. We are neither hot nor cold at any given point. We don't stand firm on one side or the other. In every way possible, we support, perpetuate, and cosign the culture of silence that leads to the destruction of our economic well-being, our communities, and ultimately our future, and then wallow in depression when the results manifest.

Of course, I have had unguarded conversations with young Africans from every corner of the continent and many of them have expressed sorrow and disappointment in the series of *"I can't believe our government leaders did or said that"*. Guess what? help is not on the way. We often go on social media sites and rant about everything we disapprove of and claim that lack of democracy is a fundamental problem in Africa that is affecting our justice systems and socio-economic structures. Yet we do little to nothing in efforts to engage the very structures that we set up and pay taxes to and demand that justice guide all their actions on our behalf.

One of the main reasons for this volume is to waken that conscious instinct in all Africans, old and young, so that we can be fed up with watching 1 billion people's interests being spiked for politics and fake patriotism to justify some very insane behaviors and ill-informed decisions by our governments and politicians. It is to this reason, and no other that I am writing. We need to self-reflect through a mirror and tackle the issues we see in us, because we have a continent to build.

National issues are complex issues that require sophisticated responses. There are still far too many men, women, and children who do not have access to good healthcare or adequate clean water and electricity supply. Too many are living with untreated social illnesses, too many are hopeless and hungry, and far too many are still living in fear and isolation as the stigma attached to being politically involved continue to permeate families and communities throughout the continent.

This literature is also a challenge to test if there is a silent majority that is willing to come together on issues that we face. We should have a healthy discussion; we do not have to resent others social values and should definitely not have religion/ethnicity be a reason for prejudice. Unfortunately, most people do not always say exactly what they mean, and often change their minds or act contradictorily. Caring about good governance is not political; it is being responsible. Otherwise, we will continue to have a very loud minority who divert national debates to promote personal agendas and put in place ineffective programs that are a waste of already scarce resources, and more soberingly, waste of lives.

Good governance is not the sole responsibility of government alone.

Far too many of us spend too much time making obscene references for being the core group of this organization or that movement; or pointing fingers and accusing others of being the main reasons why we are still a very marginally developing continent. We spend very little time engaging the very structures we established to be handling the affairs of our countries and our continent for us. Well, it doesn't matter if you're a businessman, a farmer, an educator, a student, a politician, or a mere neutral…it's five minutes to midnight, Cinderella. And it is not going to be pretty at half past the hour. If you thought times were tough within our continent, you have not seen anything yet.

I think what we the silent majority failed to convey to

our governments and our leaders is that we the *"people"* did not vote for the western countries, the oppositions, or the distractors, as our elected officials love to call them. We pay our taxes to the governments and vote for our leaderships. Therefore, being critical of our governments does not make us *"oppositions/distractors"* any more than being supportive of our government policies make us supporters of the party of the elected officials or makes us opportunists. We are Africans, meaning we only owe allegiance to her cause and absolutely nothing else. We will compliment our governments if they serve us well, and we will critique and sometimes even criticize them if they fail us.

I. Women Involvement:

No country can prosper without the involvement of women in all sectors of national development. Women participation in politics have been very limited since independence. Participation here means more than just the right to vote, but also participation in decision making, political activism, political consciousness, and so on. History has shown that women were once very involved in Africa's leadership and politics, from the various Queens (Linguerrs) of the Senegambia region, the famous Queens of Ethiopia, to traditional Queen Mothers like Yaa Asantewaa of Ghana.

The African woman has been the number one ally of the African man throughout history. They fought, bled, and died alongside their male counterparts on the battlefields for freedom, and they were forgotten as soon as we gained our independence/freedom. In 1956, over 20,000 women marched from various regions in South Africa to the apartheid capital of Pretoria to protest against the injustice of the apartheid regime. In 1951, women such as Leticia Quake, Hanna Cudjoe, Ama Nkrumah, and Madam Sophia Doku were selected by the Convention People's Party (CPP) in Ghana as propaganda secretaries. They travelled around Ghana conducting political education meetings and recruiting members for their party's struggle for independence. Kenyan women were held in detention camps during the Mau Mau rebellion for standing by their male warriors. Over 30% of the Eritrean liberation movements were made up of women during the struggle against the military junta of Mengistu Hailemariam. In Guinea Bissau and Mozambique, Titina Sila and Josina Machel both died in battlefields while serving in the liberation movements of Amilcar Cabral (of Bissau) and Samora Machel (of Mozambique). It cannot be determined during what age of our history the stigma and stereotype that women should not be involved in politics stemmed from.

Whether it is having a mere opinion or holding leadership positions and political participations, women are largely silent on the African continent. This seems to be the case even though they have proven in multiple cases that they are very capable of holding leadership positions and can become agents of change. Ellen Johnson Sirleaf of Liberia became the first woman in Africa to be elected President and brought an end to the country's long-lasting civil war. Throughout history 7 other women have been selected or constitutionally appointed presidents due to vacancy in the presidency of their respective countries. Sylvie Kinigi of Burundi, Ivy Matsepe-Casaburri of South Africa, Rose Francine Rogombe of Gabon, Agnes Monique Ohsan Bellepeau of Mauritius, Joyce Hilda Banda of Malawi, Catherine Samba Panza of Central African Republic, Ameenah Firdaus

Gurib-Fakim of Mauritius, and Sahle-Work Zewde of Ethiopia. And recently we have witnessed a surge into politics by Rwandan women. Women in Rwanda as of 2019 top the world rankings of women in National Assembly or as parliamentarians, with 51 percent of representation compared to the world average of 15.1 percent.

Despite significant progress made for women's rights, women are still confined to stereotypical gender roles in African politics. Namely campaign organizers, dancers and cheerleaders for male political leaders, cooking and catering of food and drinks during political rallies. Women continue to be constrained by religion, male patriarchy, and cultural norms that limit their participation in leadership and national issues. Women are asked and even trained to be submissive and be back benchers to their men counterparts. And those who dare to challenge the status quo are often met with insults and humiliations reminding them to stay in their lanes. Per Africa Renewal 2017 report, "women in politics", in 2015, Uganda, opposition party member named Zainab Fatima Naigaga was arrested alongside her male compatriots on their way to a political rally, but she was the only one who was stripped naked and humiliated while the men were left alone. In Nigeria, Ms. Ekwunife was demeaned and insulted during her 2011 Senate campaign for Nigeria's House of Representatives, her opponent photoshopped her picture on a naked female body and posted it on YouTube. In Rwanda, activist, Diane Shima Rwigara's candidacy for their presidential election got disqualified by election officials after naked pictures of her flooded the internet two days after she declared her candidacy. Unfortunately, some of these experiences are not unique, in fact humiliating women in politics or aspiring for political positions are common. During former president Yahya Jammeh's government in The Gambia, female members of the major opposition party, United Democratic Party (UDP), were arrested and stripped naked while being tortured by the rogue National Intelligence Agents (NIA). All these factors lead to self-apathy, self-censorship, and silence among women. And as a result, many African women lack the confidence and the competitive *"it factor"* in political arenas even in cases where they may be more qualified or possess superior ideas compared to their male counterparts. Some of the most prominent and influential women in the continent have relegated themselves as only social/ gender activist even though they can offer more. Not to say that gender activism does not play a significant role in the modern African society. I consider myself a feminist and an advocate for gender equality, but why settle for only being an activist when you can be at the decision-making table influencing decisions. Gender stereotype is a huge problem in the political sphere within the continent. But if we are to make strides in advancing the women agenda, women must muster the courage to overcome some of their fears. And "we-men" must become their allies and help them through this process.

In order to overcome the women apathy in politics and leadership in Africa, women empowerment must start in our traditional homes. The responsibility and status of our women must be improved within our households, which are usually undermined by discriminatory stereotypes and domestic violence. The socio-economic conditions of the African woman must change as well, poverty and illiteracy usually disqualify women from political participation. Politics everywhere are usually dictated by money and education, and many an African woman come up very short in both categories. Per the report of Civil Society pre-COMEDAF V meeting in Abuja, 2012, in 47 out of the 54 countries in Africa, girls usually have a measly 50% chance of completing primary school. Many statistics have shown that educated women in Africa usually have better economic conditions and are usually more politically conscious and confident in their abilities.

II. Youth Involvement:

Although Africa has the largest youthful population in the world, over 200 million people between the ages of 15 and 24, per the African Development Bank (AfDB), there is a huge political apathy among the young people of the continent. Due to the large youthful population of Africa and the high unemployment rates, many African leaders fear imminent youth uprising, and therefore strategically marginalize young people from political processes. In cases where the young people are involved, seasoned politicians often used them for selfish political agendas and inciting violence to disrupt political processes during elections. There are other factors that also contribute to the low-level youth involvement in politics in Africa such as poverty, unemployment, lack of trust in politicians, and downright lack of interest in politics and all politically related affairs.

However, in recent years we have seen some very positive activities. The emergence of Y'en a Marre (Enough is Enough) movement in Senegal, the Balai Citoyen movement in Burkina Faso, the Filimbi movement in Congo, the "Gambia Has Decided" youth movement in The Gambia, and the Youth Acting for Change programs in Mali and Togo are only a few examples. These movements, with the aim of giving African youths a voice have yielded some very promising results. But these are just few cases. The majority of our inaugural leaders were in their early twenties/thirties when they began their political struggles. Before independence, African youths were highly motivated and politically conscious, but we can't say the same post-independence.

Even though about 62% of Africa's population is under age 25 (per report on Sub-Saharan Africa by Dr. Claire Schaffnit-Chatterjee), African leaders are 42 years older than the median age of the citizens of their constituents/countries. The re-election of 76-year-old President Buhari of Nigeria and 85-year-old Paul Biya of Cameroon are a clear testament to this trend, whereas Canada and France elected 43 and 41-year-old prime minister and president respectively in the same time frame. This goes to show the general hallow division and disconnectedness in African politics.

The story of Africa is a very strange one. We cheer for the good guys in public, but we elect the bad guys in private. Professor PLO Lumumba of Kenya is well celebrated and cheered for all over Africa. He attracts packed auditoriums all across the continent, he was appointed by the Kenyan government to fight corruption in Kenya, and so he is a representation of the good guys. But when he ran for parliamentary elections, he was not elected. Some critics and observers reported that the elections were rigged. In the professor's own words, *"even if the elections were to be fair, I would have still lost the elections because people like me do not get elected in Africa"*. This is a very tragic reality in Africa. It is not the public admiration we show for people like him that moves me, but the silent endorsement we give to the bad guys that keeps me awake at night.

The silent majority must come together and speak with univocal voices to our governments and leaders about our expectations and needs. It is a responsibility and even a duty for the silent majority to be heard. We can no longer afford to remain impartial to our politics. We have a continent to build.

Chapter Four

Sports in Africa:
A Failed Endeavor

*"This may sound brutally critical, but Africa is not good at
collective winning in almost anything."*
—SAIKOU CAMARA

The tragedy of Africa is that not only have we failed at serious matters such as governance and human progress; we equally failed at the most mundane things such as sports. One of the ironies of our existence as Africans is that *"blacks"* dominate athletics around the world, and yet Africa, which is considered the primogenitor of the black race, performs abysmally in athletics. Why? Africa's bane is that we are abound in raw talent, minerals, and so forth, but fail woefully to nurture or refine these to enhance their value. Everything of value requires refinement to attain its true significance. There is no consensus, no obvious explanation, and no single unified theories why African athletes underperform in international competitions and on the world stage.

There are number of theories that we can look into though. One of them is that Africa as a continent, and Africans as a people have more pressing issues and concerns to deal with than sports. Sport is not a priority for many African parents and their kids. When I was a child, we had a song we used to sing which says, *"Learning is better than silver and goal"*. My parents would punish me when I go outside to play soccer instead of studying my lessons. Sports is a numbers game in Africa; out of every tens of thousands of athletes, only a few may get lucky and become successful. This demoralized many African parents from encouraging their children to pursue professional careers in sports. Whereas in the west, children are encouraged by their parents to join sport academies and after school athletic programs at a very early age. This can be done not only for athletic reasons, but to also nurture their leadership and teamwork spirit.

Poor infrastructure and poor governance are also contributing factors that affect not only sports but everything from public health to education to opportunities for advancement. There is also an issue of *"economic safety net"* that affects African athletes. An athlete in America can go back to school and seek for good paying jobs and become a middle-class citizen if their pursuit of an athletic career fails to matriculate into success. But an African athlete does not have such luxury; they may never recover from all of the lost time they didn't spend in school or laboring at some job.

However, the purpose of this literature is not to analyze the things that are out of our reach/control as a continent. Rather the things we are doing or not doing that are hindering our success. I will reflect on our performance at the FIFA soccer/football World Cups and the Olympics.

I. FIFA World Cups: Football/Soccer

From legendary Cameroon striker Roger Milla's hip shake in 1990 to Rashidi Yekini's (RIP) unforgettable celebration after scoring the Super Eagles' first ever FIFA world cup goal in 1994 to Papa Bouba Diop of Senegal's sole goal that sank France in 2002, Africans' excitement about FIFA World Cups are always short lived. Though soccer is the most popular sports in the continent, our participation in soccer world cup games are just for sideshows and participation purposes only. We are the ugly friend that the beautiful girl brings with her to parties just so that she won't be alone. The story is always the same, one African country will become the element of surprise in the tournament, win few significant games until their inevitable exit after the group stages. The question becomes, why have African teams underperformed on the sport's biggest stage, despite the skills and talent of African players?

This may sound brutally critical, but Africa is not good at collective winning in almost anything. There is no single or certain answer as to why, but the continent's heartbreakingly poor performance in the 2014 soccer World Cup highlighted some of the hindrances to our success that I will highlight. Although African teams have been consistently competing in Soccer World Cups since 1982 (Algeria and Cameroon), no African team has ever made it to the semi-final stages of the competition. I must note that Egypt was the first African team to qualify for the world cup tournament in Italy, 1934.

2010 showed a lot of optimism with the continent hosting its first ever Soccer World Cup tournament in South Africa. During the first-round games, many commentators and analysts were heard saying that this was the first time the tournament had 6 African teams in the competition. Playing in Africa was considered by many spectators as an opportunity for African teams to end their abysmal luck in the tournament's history. But just like many competitions before it, African teams under-performed. It must be noted that African soccer players are very skilled and talented. African soccer players are among some of the best players in the best soccer leagues around the world. The three top scorers in the English Premier League for 2018/19 season are all African players, Mohamed Salah of Egypt, Pierre-Emerick Aubameyang of Gabon, and Sadio Mane of Senegal. The 2018 world cup champions, the French team are a great example of this. Wherein 50 percent of their starting eleven players were of African descents, and 80 percent of their entire team were either directly from or of African descent. Therefore, looking at our collective team accolades will be a poor measuring tool of African athletic talents and skills. So how else can we explain our failures in our collective team sports? Let us take a look.

It is fair to say that African teams have been on the receiving end of unsportsmanlike conducts in the competition's history. For instance, in the case of Algeria in 1982, they competed very well and won two out of their 3 games, beating Germany and Chile and losing to Austria. A draw or a win for a strong Austrian side against Germany was going to secure Algeria's advancement from the group stages, but Austria instead had a gentleman's agreement with Germany and decided to not compete at the highest level against Germany and settle for a 1-nil defeat knowing that that will be sufficient for both teams to advance into the next rounds and eliminate Algeria. I am aware of the fact that the attitudes of the soccer authorities towards African teams are sometimes questionable at best.

Player strikes due to multiple reasons, pay disputes between players and sport authorities, infighting, match fixings, disagreement between African big players and their sporting authorities/officers, lack of resources, and lack of professionalism, have impaired African teams at the big stages.

Of the 5 African teams that qualified for Brazil, 2014, 3 were involved in player pay disputes with their respective soccer governing authorities. Cameroonian players led by their star player Samuel Eto'o, refused to board their scheduled flight to a game in Rio de Janeiro without their allowances paid up front. This caused them to arrive late to the tournament. After they qualified from the group stages and onto the knockout rounds, Nigerian national team had to cancel a training session to catch the attention of their authorities to issue their bonus payments. Ghana, the biggest embarrassment in the tournament, had to fly in 3 million US dollars into Rio before their players agreed to play a single game. While other nations were physically and mentally getting prepared for the world's biggest competition, African teams were fighting over money. Sometimes it seems like we have a self-destruct button that we press anytime something positive is about to happen for the continent. Why is paying the wages of our soccer players an issue? Samuel Eto'o was once quoted saying that *our leaders do not respect us. Until we are respected, other continent will never have any consideration for us.* This only went further to show the lack of respect for our professional athletes. Some may argue that patriotism should come first in such matters. But like I always remind people, patriotism does not put food on the table or shelter over someone's head. Their livelihood depends on them playing soccer and they deserve to be adequately compensated even if they represent their countries.

On the flip side, there is also a lack of professionalism exercised by some African soccer professionals when representing their national teams. Like in the case of Cameroon Assou-Ekotto head-butting his own teammate, Benjamin Moukandjo, during their 4-0 defeat to Croatia in the 2014 World Cup. That was perhaps the most embarrassing moment of the tournament, at least from the perspective of African soccer. Teammates usually work together to face their opponents, but African players sometimes head-butt each other instead of the soccer ball. Ghana also lost two of their best players in the middle of the 2014 tournament in Brazil due to physical and verbal altercation between players and team officials. Some wealthy African players have no regard for their coaches or national team officials whom they see as inferior to their own celebrity status. They do not respect team policies such as curfews, training schedules, meal plans, and so on. African players must show the same amount of professionalism and discipline for their countries that they show when representing their European clubs. African teams showed very little class and professionalism in Rio, 2014. It is one thing to lose with dignity to a better team, but it is a shame to lose due to lack of professionalism.

Before the 2014 World Cup in Brazil, the Ghana Football Association was indicted for agreeing to take part in international football matches organized by match fixers. Both in 2010 and 2014 World Cups, Nigeria was involved in match fixing scandals during friendly matches prior to the big occasions. And many soccer analysts alleged that some of the African professional soccer players are usually paid off in high profile soccer matches to allow easy goals for their opponents or make silly tackles that will lead to their dismissal from games to allow their opponents a competitive advantage. They said this is because many African players do not get paid much to represent their national teams. Though some of these claims are difficult to prove, it is hard to dismiss them especially when very good African teams lose carelessly in World Cup games against teams that many analysts considered the African teams to be the favorites. How can our national teams win when they place personal interest before national interest? Corruption is the deadliest disease in the African continent since we obtained our independence, and it affects even our sports men and women.

Former Liberia international player and current president, George Weah, who was named FIFA World Player of the year in 1995, said another problem is the issue of poor governing bodies that are put in charge of soccer federations in Africa. He stated, *"Former players govern European football while those without passion or knowledge of the game rule in Africa. Footballers rather than officials should travel business class on flights because they are the one[s] going to play"*. There is an African proverb that you cannot become a professor in a subject matter that you have never been a student of. In many African countries, appointments/selections of sport authorities are made via political appointments and affiliations. People who have little to no interest or knowledge about sporting activities are put in charge to govern sports. If you hire a mechanic to conduct open heart surgery on your patient, then you must buy a coffin and prepare to bury your corpse.

All of these issues mentioned are avoidable and self-inflicting obstacles that we can improve on.

II. Olympic Games:

With every Olympic Games, new heroes and role models are born. And the 2012 Olympic games were no different, whether it was the story of Mo Farah of Britain, who came to the UK as a refugee when he was ten years old and ended up winning 2 gold medals for his host nation; the story of Oscar Pistorius, 100m sprinter from South Africa, who got both his legs amputated when he was only 11 months old; or the story of American 400m relay sprinter Manteo Mitchell, who broke his leg while running the 400m relay semi-final and struggle to limp his way to the finish line in agony and refused to quit on his teammates and country …truly inspiring. These are some of the reasons why we all love sports, the greatly moving stories, and the unbelievable achievements by those we cheer for.

We witnessed similar great moments during the Rio 2016 Olympics. We saw for the first time 10 refugee athletes, who were forced to flee their homes because of civil wars or political persecution, get cheered on enthusiastically by the crowds as they participated and marched under the Olympic flag. We witnessed two of once-in-a-lifetime legends, Michael Phelps and Usain Bolt both mesmerized us with their greatness as they wave goodbye to the competition in grand style. And how could we forget the Samaritan gesture we witness displayed during the women's 5000M heat when Nikki Hamblin of New Zealand and Abbey D'Agostino from the U.S. got tangled up and fell. They supported and encouraged each other as they struggle to the finish line, reminding all of us that there is more to the Olympics than just winning medals, our humanity.

Some people raised eyebrows to the increased number of European and American athletes with African names. I personally do not have much issue with athletes of African descent representing their host nations in the Olympic Games. But my concern is, will gold for guys like Mo Farah (in the Olympics) encourage more African athletes to become foreign nationals or will it encourage more children in Somalia to aspire to become the next Mo Farah for Somalia? I will leave that for history to judge.

However, this chapter is not about the Mo Farahs' of our continent but rather about the likes of Suwaibou Sanneh of The Gambia who decided to stay (for now) to represent our continent and how we can help to develop them for the 2020 and future Olympics to come.

South Africa (6 medals), Ethiopia (7 medals), and Kenya (11 medals) had won most medals at the Olympics in the African contest during the 2012 Olympic. Their athletes were phenomenal, their Olympic programs ran deep, and they ruled the long- and middle-distance events. South Africa had the biggest squad going to the London Olympics, and they improved on their single medal count in Beijing (2008). The most inspiring story for the African continent was the 400m runner from South Africa who qualified for the Olympics, Oscar Pistorius. He is a double amputee who runs on blades instead of feet; truly amazing (unfortunately for him he is currently serving a 13 years prison term for the murder of his fiancé).

In Rio 2016, African countries improved their medal counts to 45, making it the continent's most successful Olympics in history. 11 African countries contributed to the medal count. Kenya led by winning 13 medals (six gold, six silver, and one bronze). South Africa improved from Beijing 2008 and London 2012 by surpassing Ethiopia on their medal count. South African athletes, Caster Semenya and Wayde van Niekerk wowed the world with their record breaking and historic wins. Overall the continent won a total of 5% of the medals, with the largest share of the 48% going to European teams, America's won 22%, and Asia winning 21%. A continent of one billion people, constituting 17% of total world population, winning merely 5% can be seen as an improvement compared to our past Olympic experiences. Nonetheless, it is as disappointing as our previous experiences.

The rest of the reports were filled with disappointments and very forgettable memories such as; African athletes going AWOL even before the closing ceremony of the games. Very embarrassing, but yet I cannot blame them. The African continent was poorly represented on the medal chart yet again. We the spectators jumped to our feet and celebrated in the mere sighting of our national flags on our colored TV's and updated our social media profiles with praises for our athletes even when they came dead last (no pun intended). Our levels of expectations were so depressingly low and unbearable to watch sometimes. We vilified anyone who dare criticize our performance and the lack of preparedness of our athletes in the name of *"country"*. We beat our chests and label ourselves as patriots all over social networking sites just because we wrote, *"Go…insert African country name here"*. But don't get me wrong; this is not a lashing out at our sportsmen and women who left everything they got on the tracks/fields for the flags they represented (ignoring those who disappeared even before their events). But all of us cannot be so-called *"good patriots"* if we want things to change in future Olympics. Somebody has to take the name calling and say the unpopular things if we want to improve. No, I am not trying to be a hero; I just don't appreciate mediocrity very well. Participation alone is no longer enough; we also need to start thinking about winning or not losing, however you look at it.

I am not ignorant about the realities Africa is faced with and the issues hindering our performances in all sporting activities. I do not think we have the time and resources to organize for more sports. The priorities for most African governments should be the provision of food, security, shelter, education, and healthcare for their teeming populations. Obtaining synchronized swimming medal sounds so good to the ears but at this point it is very tantalizing to an average African country. I'm just *"keeping it real"*. The biggest problem that hinders African nations from being competitive in sport is poverty (some people may cite the case of Jamaica to refute this claim, but the variables are different). Unlike in the U.S., Britain, and China where sports are well funded by government and well-wishers/donors, sporting in Africa is an individual struggle. Just as we have failed in political leadership, we are failing in all categories of organized anything. For better results in sports, countries must do a lot more and give support to various sporting activities. I am not only talking about financial support. I will try to concentrate on less financial assistance African countries can embark on to improve their chances in future competitions.

A. Champions are made in the Gym:

There is an old African proverb that *"you can't fatten the pig on market day"*. Medals are won in the practice gym. A renowned African American Boxer, Joe Frazier, once said, *"Champions are not made in the ring; they are merely recognized there."* Africa, like our natural resources, we leave our talents unrefined. Talent alone is not adequate for attaining success in any discipline. Many years of training, according to a scientifically measurable regimen, is the only way to prime up our contestants to the point where they can favorably compete with their counterparts from other continents. We provide very little or no training for our athletes. Many African athletes participate in less than two competitive competitions in an entire year. Athletes need to compete continuously to stay motivated and hungry else forget about winning. Ethiopian swimmer, Robel Habte, was mocked on social media (during the 2016 Olympic Games) with many calling him *"Robel the Whale"* for his protruding paunch. Watching him stand next to the other swimmers, it looked like the American popular prank show, *"Punk'd"*, on MTV. His destiny to get last position was already predetermined even before he jumped into the pool.

In the case of female athletes, to be honest I lost all hopes even before majority of them took their first step during the Olympic Games; and I consider myself an optimist. I don't think that their competitors were better/faster than them or more talented than them, but it was evident that they were more skilled than our African female athletes. Those other women looked like *"terminators"*; it was evident that they were better prepared than our women. We cannot wait until two weeks before major competitions to start paying attention to our sports men/women. I don't think it will require a national budget to provide them with free gym memberships, free medical assistance to all national health medical facilities, timely energy supplement food supplies, free training materials (running shoes/gears), free physical health consultants, knowledgeable coaches, organize local sporting activities to keep athletes motivated and competitive year round, seek for local/international sponsorships on their behalf to attend sporting competitions (money will not be coming out of government pockets)…etc. Many of these things for the most part are already available, and it is only a matter of getting them to the athletes.

It is no coincidence that many of the acknowledged African athletes are based in the West where they live and train. Most of the African athletes who remain on the continent have to first overcome logistics and infightings from the very organization that are setup to support them before they even compete against their actual opponents. In my opinion, the politics within our sporting committees are a bigger problem than lack of resources. We cannot wait until the Olympic Games come around every four years before we celebrate and support our athletes. The outpour of love and praise from Africans all around the world for their athletes was really nice, but it won't hurt to start celebrating them and making them our national heroes; publish their accomplishments on magazines and billboards, offer them media advertisement to help them support their families (it's not free money they will be offering services).

B. Create More Awareness:

I am convinced that many Africans like myself have watched the 2012 and 2016 summer Olympics in London/Rio and found coverage of events we never knew existed. My outrage is how can you compete for a medal in a sport you didn't even know existed in the first place? African countries are doing a horrible job in promoting non-traditional sporting events. In my home country I know of hundreds of people who can swim from Africa to Asia effortlessly (yes, I am exaggerating it). Educating people about sporting events they do for fun every day is not a million-dollar expenditure. Creating awareness on non-traditional sports like table tennis, judo, taekwondo, swimming, walkathon, badminton, cycling, wrestling, boxing, and so on can provide African nations with more representation to compete on the world stage. And you will be surprised how cost effective some of these individual sporting events are compared to team sports.

C. Athletic Scholarships:

If we don't do anything else ... Please let us pay attention to this one thing, *"scholarship programs"*. This is the most prudent and yielding program for African athletes. Call it a shortcut if you may. We can develop and improve our athletes both physically and academically. Yes, we can have our cake and eat it too. We need to help our athletes to secure athletic scholarship programs in colleges and universities around the world. Invite university recruiters to our local and international sporting events, help distribute video tapes and picture images of our athletes to college and university recruiters and provide information centers regarding college funding applications for our athletes. These things work, and I have the facts to prove it. By the way let me digress here for a minute. Whoever came up with this silly phrase that *"you can't have your cake and eat it"*? Nonsense! This comment is only for the have NOTs. If you have enough cake you can eat all the cake you want, and you will still have enough left. Anyway, back to the Olympics.

Suwaibou Sanneh, a 100m sprinter from The Gambia, qualified for the semi-finals of the 100m race which featured the likes of Tyson Gay, Usain Bolt, and Yohan Blake in London. Many of my readers don't even know that Suwaibou was at the Beijing Olympics (2008) as well and he didn't even qualify through the second round. However, after four years of training in Jamaica, not only did he pass through to the second rounds, he broke a national record set by then Gambian sprinter, Jaysuma Saidy Ndure (Now Norwegian citizen), in the process. And if we continue to ignore our athletes, we will lose more of them just like we did Ndure.

Charlton Nyirenda and Joyce Tafatatha of Malawi equally enjoyed their first swim in a heated 50m pool at the University of Gloucestershire (UK) where they attended college few weeks ahead of the London Olympic Games as part of their Olympic preparations (without a single indoor pool in Malawi). In case you are wondering; yes, we have swimming pools in Africa, but they usually exist to entertain Caucasian tourists from richer/western countries. And as for the rivers and lakes - they are sometimes infested with man-eating crocodiles and hippos, and deadly diseases. So why not ship our talented kids to western universities where they can practice and get some education while they are at it? Do you remember Kirani James? The

400m gold medalist from Grenada...He was developed and trained at the University of Alabama. And I can go on and on with similar stories from Nigeria to Jamaica. We lack the resources and time to train them ourselves so why not...?

D. Keep politics away from sports:

Politics should in no way influence sports because it destroys the fundamental nature of sports. There is a huge difference between governments being supportive versus being intrusive. It's a thin line, and it shouldn't be crossed.

After the 2004 Anthem games, the Tanzanian athletes, who won not a single medal, were greeted by newspaper headlines demanding an explanation for the country's poor performance and calling for the minister of sports to apologize to the nation. Yet we wonder why more African athletes are choosing to represent their Western host countries.

Uganda has failed to qualify several of their athletes for the London Olympics, because the stadium they should have used to record their time trials was hosting a Japanese Happy Science Religious Convention, backed by the government (true story, Google it). I don't know if I should laugh out loud or yell out a curse word. What a great encouragement for their athletes (you are welcome to insert an eye rolling emoji here). Excuse me and let me digress here once again. I think *"GoogleIt"* should be a word in the dictionary, and I will volunteer to provide the definition. Think about it, how many times do you use the phrase *"Google it"*...okay back to this.

And in The Gambia, in 2004, during the London Olympic Games, the Gambian athletes and officials were made to wear colors matching the color (green) of the political party (APRC) of the then president Yahya Jammeh. Which backfired and became a major turnoff for the Gambian spectators. A moment of unity and patriotism turned into a partisan jamboree and a missed opportunity. Sport officials were also selected and elected based on their affiliation and support for the then APRC government. Corrupt officials who had the aegis of president Jammeh or his government went unpunished. And parts of the country that are suspected to be opposition party strongholds were denied supporting amenities and supplies such as soccer balls, sponsored tournaments, trophies, and the like.

The bottom line is our athletes need a collective support, and politics take away this much-needed support, starting from donors, fans, and well-wishers. If people do not feel represented, they will not give their blessings in any form.

Chapter Five

Our Heroes' Stories: Saints or Sinners?

*"If your actions create a legacy that inspires others to dream
more, learn more, do more and become more, then,
you are an excellent leader."*
—DOLLY PARTON

There was a time when Africans thought colonialism and feudalism were our problems, and I must say rightly so, colonialism and feudalism systems were in fact problems. We fought against them and established our own African governments and we sang and danced with joy for freedom. We introduced socialism as our systems of government; Ghana under Nkrumah had a socialist government, Tanzania under the leadership of Nyerere had a socialist government, Kenya under the leadership of Kenyatta had a socialist government, Zambia under the leadership of Kaunda had a socialist government, Guinea Conakry under the leadership of Sekou Toure had a socialist government, Mali under the leadership of Modibo Keita had a socialist government, as well as many other African countries post-independence. Our socialist governments failed, and we thought they were the root cause of our problems. Our military generals picked up arms against our governments and overthrew them and their socialist ideas. We sang freedom songs and danced for joy for our uniformed men and women and their revolutionary ideas. Our military governments also failed, and we thought the military generals and their revolutionary ideas were our problems. We formed rebel groups and grassroots movement and engaged them in arm struggles and popular uprisings to defeat them. We once again composed heroic songs and sang and danced and established democratic governments. Our democratic governments are failing us in many parts of the continent, now we are going for elections and screaming for change and term limits from every corner of the continent. Africans are never short of identifying our continent's problems and implementing solutions that prove to be problems themselves. The questions now become what is Africa's problem and what does Africa want? These are very instigating questions but ones that must be asked. First, we must look back at our history and evaluate the lives of our great African leaders; learn from their good ideas and try to right some of their shortcomings as we move forward.

I. The Nkrumah Story:

Accra, the capital city of former Gold Coast and present-day Ghana, is believed to have been derived from the word "*nkran*" meaning ants in Akan. In its streets walked Kwame Nkrumah, a great man who led Ghana's struggle for independence. He led Ghana to economic success during the nation's early days, founded the Kwame Nkrumah University of Science and Technology, and played a very important role in the inception of the Organization of African Unity (OAU) in Addis Ababa, Ethiopia. He is well known for his Pan African vision of let there be no North Africa, East Africa, South Africa, or West Africa, but one Africa.

Kwame Nkrumah was born on September 21st, 1909, in Nkroful village. His father, Opanyin Kofi Nwiana Ngolomah, was a goldsmith by profession and his mother, Madam Elizabeth Nyaniba, was a farmer and a petty trader. He attended the prestigious Achimota College in 1930, which was founded by former colonial rulers in 1927, and became a teacher upon graduation. At the age of 26, in 1935, he left Ghana for the United States and attended Lincoln University, Pennsylvania.

The Marcus Garvey and W.E.B Dubois Pan African movement influenced Nkrumah and the socialist philosophy of Karl Marx, which motivated him to join the 5th Pan African Congress in 1945, held in Manchester, United Kingdom. During that congress they accelerated the struggle for self-rule in Africa. Upon his return to Ghana after 12 years, he became the secretary general of the first political party, United Gold Coast Convention (UGCC), whose founding members were later known as the Big Six. In 1951, he formed his own political party, Convention People's Party (CPP), and became Ghana's first prime minister. And in 1957, as the prime minister, he led Ghana to independence. Ghana was the first African nation to gain independence from British colonial rule. Nkrumah was quoted in his independence speech saying that *"Ghana's independence will be meaningless if other African countries are not free and independent"*. On that same year, 1957, he married a young Egyptian woman, Fathia. He was blessed with four children: Francis, Gamal, Samia, and Sekou (namesake of former president of Guinea, Sekou Toure).

During his term as president of Ghana, Kwame Nkrumah introduced a one-party state, which led to many of his critics considering him as a dictator. Some closed affiliates of Nkrumah reported that that decision was born out of necessity. They said Nkrumah established a lot of institutions, and the majority of the people capable of running those institutions were all members of the oppositions. Passing a constitutional one-party state was implemented to coil self-apathy of the few educated elites who would have chosen to be opposition members instead of public servants. This backfired and caused more agitation and resistance among opposition groups. Due to the increase in opposition groups against his government, Nkrumah later introduced the *"detention act"* via parliament, which allowed the state to detain anyone incommunicado indefinitely without any charges. Many critics believed that as his decisions and actions became more dictatorial, his own party members began to turn against him. He survived five assassination attempts on his life including his own security guard firing a gun at him at his residence. And in August of 1962, as he was returning from Upper Volta, present day Burkina Faso, a grenade hidden in a bucket of flowers allegedly planted for him exploded and left a little girl dead.

Despite the increased numbers in opposition groups, Nkrumah managed to stay in power until the Ghana economy began to deplete as the prices of cocoa started going down in the world market. Vibrant state enterprises started to collapse, and food prices inflated. Ghana went from having the highest per capita income in Africa to a barely surviving economy. Ghanaians began to question the methods of their one-time beloved leader as the economy continued to worsen. Many experts believe the turning point and the final nail into his government's coffin came when he donated 10 million British pounds from the coffers of Ghana to Guinea Conakry, under the leadership of President Sekou Touré. This philanthropic gesture didn't sit well with many Ghanaians. On the 21st of Feb 1966, he boarded a plane heading to Vietnam on a peace mission; his government got overthrown 3 days later. In the morning of 24th Feb 1966, the self-proclaimed *"President for life"*, Nkrumah was overthrown in a military coup led by Emmanuel Kwasi Kotoka and the National Liberation Council. Many international observers and Nkrumah himself alleged that the American CIA conspired in the coup, as stated in his 1969 Memoir *"Dark Days in Ghana"*.

Kwame Nkrumah went into exile in Guinea Conakry with his family and got appointed a co-president of Guinea by his comrade, President Sekou Touré. Many critics saw that as undemocratic in itself and many Guineans disagreed with the appointment. In April of 1972, while on a medical trip to Romania, Africa lost a true son and visionary leader. The medical reports said that he died of prostate cancer, but some people, including Amilcar Cabral, former freedom fighter of Cape Verde, said that Nkrumah died of *"cancer of betrayal."* For a man who survived 5 assassination attempts and had the CIA allegedly involved in overthrowing his government, it is hard to dismiss the claims that he might have been poisoned, but there is no tangible evidence to these claims.

II. The Nyerere Story:

Tanzania is not only known for its wilderness, wild animals, and beautiful landscape, it is home to one of the greatest sons of the continent of Africa. Kambarage (Julius) Nyerere was born on the 13th of April 1922, in Tanganyika. His father, Nyerere Burito, the chief of the Zanaki ethnic group had 26 children. He received a scholarship at the Makerere University in Kampala, Uganda, where he graduated in 1947 with a teaching diploma. He received a government scholarship in 1949 to attend the University of Edinburgh where he obtained a Master of Arts degree in Economics and History in 1952. It was during his studies in Edinburgh that he encountered the Fabian Society socialist organization, which would later influence his political ideology and system of governance.

Nyerere led his people into a violence-free struggle to independence and became Tanzania's first President. Mwalimu (teacher in Swahili), as his people fondly called him, was a teacher by profession. The colonial rulers became aware of his political activism and gave him an ultimatum to either continue his teaching profession or become a politician. He was reported to have said that he was a schoolmaster by choice and a politician by accident. He often travelled around the country talking to people and tribal chiefs about the need for self-rule. He used his charismatic personality and charming ideas to convince the British Governor to allow elections for independence. On Dec 9th, 1961, Tanzania became a sovereign nation and a republic in 1962. Just like Nkrumah, Nyerere also implemented a one-party state, and a *"preventive detention"* act to eliminate trade unions and opposition parties. He ran for 5 elections unopposed until 1985 when he retired from public office.

As a former educator and an admirer of the Fabian movement in the UK, Mwalimu never lost his vision for education and socialism. His personal library had over 8,000 books ranging from science, arts, economics, agriculture, to religion, and so on. He was quoted as saying *"education has to increase men's physical and mental freedom ..."* He prioritized education as his government's number one agenda. He put in place an education policy called *"education for self-reliance"* to ensure that all Tanzanian children have equal access to free education. People who knew him and were close to him also described him as a man who loved and appreciate African arts.

Nyerere implemented an economic policy that many experts described as a socialist economy. In 1967, he also implemented an agricultural program called *"Ujaama"*, meaning family-hood in Swahili, to encourage his citizens to go back to their lands and farm in the form of cooperatives. While this saw the production of tea and other cash crops increase, the idea itself yielded very little result in alleviating poverty in Tanzania. Over 10 million people were voluntarily and involuntarily dispersed and resettled. Opposing villages were burned down and villagers who resisted were sometimes met with death. Tanzania faced food shortages and some critics reported that Nyerere deliberately forbade his country from importing foreign goods just so they can improve their local production. By the time he retired from public office, Nyerere left Tanzania as one of the poorest and most foreign-dependent nations in Africa.

> *"No nation has the right to make*
> *decisions for another nation ..."*

Nyerere is, however, credited for defeating Idi Amin's tyrannical army in 1979. The war, which was later known as the *"Uganda War"* was fought between Uganda and Tanzania between 1978 and 1979. After Amin seized power from Uganda's former president, Milton Obote, Nyerere provided him and few of his loyalists who fled with him a safe refuge in Tanzania. This didn't sit well with Amin as he blamed Tanzania and Nyerere for backing and supporting his enemies. Amin declared a war against Tanzania and captured some parts of Tanzania that he claimed belong to Uganda. Nyerere responded with a counter attack of his own. In a matter of few weeks Tanzania expanded its army from 40,000 to 100,000 troops ready to go to war. That war coupled with other economic crises brought Tanzania's economy to its knees.

Similar to Nkrumah, Nyerere was a die-hard supporter of African liberation and Pan Africanism. He welcomed African freedom fighters from all parts of the continent into Tanzania in the 60's and 70's. He also played an important role in the formation of the OAU in 1963. He is praised for playing a major role in the *"frontline states"* federation that led to the independence of Zimbabwe and Namibia. Many critics found it ironical that for a man who won his nation independence for his people peacefully, he was very vital in the arm struggle for independence in Zimbabwe, Namibia, and South Africa.

In 1999, one of Africa's most respected figures died of Leukemia in a London hospital. His legacy will forever be remembered in Tanzania and throughout the African continent for generations to come.

As I write this literature, it saddens my heart that for people, Nkrumah and Nyerere, who married into and dedicated their lives to Africa, lived for Africa, and died with the love of Africa in their hearts, to take their last breaths in the land of the colonizers, due to lack of proper health facilities and expertise within our continent. This is a very sad and tragic reality and an indictment to our continent. But as Nyerere himself have said, you can criticize yourself but don't do it too much until you despair, because to despair is an unforgivable sin. Therefore, I won't despair, I am still hopeful that our continent's better days are ahead of us.

III. The Nelson "Madiba" Mandela Story:

Home to the Zulu tribe and cultured people, in this same land walked great men like Shaka Zulu, King of the Mthethwa Empire, and freedom fighters such as Steve Biko. A beautiful country with a beautiful landscape and a very rich African culture is well known around the world for the Apartheid Regime. But modern-day South Africa is mostly known for one of her greatest sons, Nelson Mandela. The man the world got to know as Mandela was born with the name Rolihlahla Mandela. He was born on the 18 of July 1918 into the Madiba clan, in Mvezo village. He was born to mother, Nonqaphi Nosekeni, and father, Nkosi Mphakanyiswa Gadla Mandela. In accordance with the customs of giving all schoolchildren *"Christian Names"* during the Apartheid regime, Mandela's elementary school teacher, Miss Mdingane, gave him the name Nelson at Qunu primary school. Young Mandela attended the University College of Fort Hare, seeking his bachelor's (BA) degree in Arts, but he got expelled for joining a student protest. He eventually completed his BA at the University of South Africa in Johannesburg and later went back to Fort Hare for his graduation in 1943.

Young Mandela first entered politics when he helped form the African National Congress Youth League (ANCYL) in 1942. He slowly rose through the ranks of the ANC to becoming one of its most formidable and influential members. Many experts reported that the ANC became more radicalized under his leadership.

While facing a Treason Trial, Mandela, married a young social worker, Winnie Madikizela, on June 14, 1958. They had two daughters, Zenani and Zindziswa. He had four other children from a previous marriage, Makaziwe, Madiba Thembekile, Lewanika, and Makaziwe (who shared the same name with her sister).

Using the alias, David Motsamayi, in January of 1962, Mandela discretely got out of South Africa amid intense political tension and travelled to many African countries and the United Kingdom, seeking support for an arm struggle against the Apartheid regime. He received some military training in Morocco and Ethiopia before his return to South Africa. After 6 months of absence from South Africa, Mandela was arrested upon his return. He was charged and sentenced to 5 years in prison for leaving South Africa, while on trial, without a permit, and inciting civil disobedience among labor unions.

A month later, while serving his 5-year sentence, the apartheid regime raided the ANC headquarters and arrested several of Mandela's comrades. On a trial that came to be known as the Rivonia trial, on Oct 9, 1963, Mandela and 10 other members of the ANC party were tried for sabotage of the apartheid regime. Knowing that the odds were stacked up against them and they might have to face the death penalty by execution, with life sentence being the least possible outcome, Mandela and his colleagues implemented an unconventional defense mechanism. They used the witness box as their political podium to announce their political agenda to the world. On April 20th, 1964, on the dock of the courthouse, he delivered his famous speech, *"I have fought against white domination and I have fought against black domination. I have cherished the idea of a democratic and free society in which all persons live together in harmony and with equal opportunities. It is an idea, which I hope to live for and to achieve. But if need be, it is an idea for which I am prepared to die"*. On June 11, 1964, Mandela and seven other accused members of the ANC were found guilty and sentenced to life in prison with hard labor.

"I went for a long holiday for 27 years", Mandela was once quoted saying about his time in prison. But the realities are far from any sort of holiday experience. When he and his comrades first arrived in Robben Island prison camp, a prison warden was quoted saying to him *"this is the Island. This is where you will die"*. He wrote in his autobiography *"The Long Walk to Freedom"*, that both he and his comrades were often brandished with dehumanizing treatments. Prisoner 46664, as he was known during his time in Robben Island, was often put in solitary confinement for being defiant in prison. Both his mother and first child died while he was incarcerated, and he was denied the chance to attend their burials. His comrades said that that had a special effect on Mandela. He will recite the poem *"Invictus"*, by Ernest Henley, everyday just to uplift his spirit and maintain his sanity.

After spending 27 years in prison, on Sunday, 11 February 1990, Mandela walked out of the prison gates as a free man. He continued his pursuit to end white minority domination. He negotiated for a reconciliatory treaty that many international experts believed prevented an imminent civil war. President FW de Klerk of the Apartheid regime agreed to an all-inclusive democratic election. Almost 20 million South Africans voted in the April 27th, 1994 elections. The ANC party, with Mandela as its leader won 62% of the votes. On 10th of May 1994, South Africa inaugurated its first black President. Apartheid was officially over; South Africa was officially considered free. A one-time political prisoner became the most powerful person in South Africa.

Mandela made it a priority that South Africa's new constitution will not only benefit the ANC party, but the entire nation. He was able to reunite his rainbow nation under one flag and constitution that was inclusive of every South African, irrespective of race or economic class. Building a nation savaged by 350 years of Apartheid rule would soon prove to be difficult for its great leader. But with Mandela as its new leader there was a sense of optimism.

In the history of politics, no politician's image is ever left spotless, and Mandela was to be no different. Critics have criticized Mandela for his subtle approach and negotiation for reconciliation, his unceremonious divorce with Winnie Mandela, his romance with other women, his failure to end economic apartheid in South Africa, and so on. Other freedom fighters during the Apartheid regime also expressed some resentment for not being properly recognized for the roles they played to end the Apartheid regime. Some of these criticisms are valid, not to say that any of them are invalid. Mandela was not alone, and he had never claimed to have done it all alone. Men like Steve Biko paid the ultimate price, death. Others such as Ahmed Kathrada,

Winnie Mandela, Govan Mbeki and Walter Sisulu equa
fought with fortitude and they never despaired.

Black South Africans were also looking at the economic cake of their new country that was still far-fetched. The
nation was still divided. The schools were still divided. The
income gap seems to have widened. There was a new South
Africa for the world to admire, and there was a more som-
ber South Africa for the blacks. As in the case of an informal
settlement in the outskirts of Cape Town nicknamed *"Barcelona"*. The people, who voluntarily settle there by choice,
or lack of choice, consider themselves as the *"forgotten people"*; forgotten by the centralized political system of South
Africa. They are the people who do not identify themselves
with the South Africa that Mandela freed from the Apartheid regime. *"Barcelona"* is savaged with prostitution, violence, drugs, poverty, and crimes. They do not fit in the new
Cinderella story that South Africa is trying to sell to the
world. But *"Barcelona"*, like many other black settlements in
South Africa, is devastated with poverty. Only 30% of the
South African population controls the economic cake of the
country. Poverty is still borderline based on race: blacks and
whites. This economic disparity led to the 2015 Xenophobia
in South Africa that left about 5 foreigners dead and thousands displaced.

Mandela was a man of deep commitments, principles,
and compassion; a leader who lived for his people and was
ready to die for their cause if it were necessary. He went to
jail as a young militant and came out as a seasoned reconciliatory leader of ideas and differences. In 1999 after just one
term Mandela stood down from presidency, but he never
stopped working for the country he loved until the day he
took his last breath on December 5, 2013 at his home in

urg. Mandela is gone, but South Africa belongs
Africans. And anywhere Mandela fell short in
eir expectations; it is now their responsibility to
eir rebuilding process.

IV. The Thomas Sankara Story:

Ouagadougou, which means, *"you are welcome here at home with us"*, is the capital city of the land of Upright People, Burkina Faso. Burkina is believed to have been the capital state of the former great Songhai Empire in the 15th century under the leadership of Sunni Ali and Askia Muhammad. The country that was once known as Upper Volta is located at the south of the Sahara Desert with a population of 17.3 million people. It gained its independence from colonial France on the 5th of August 1960.

In this ancient historic region was born a revolutionary leader name Thomas Isidore Noel Sankara, former president of Burkina Faso. He was born on the 21st of December 1949, in Yako, Upper Volta, present day Burkina Faso. He was born to catholic parents, Marguerite Sankara and Sambo Joseph Sankara. He will later be known as the *"Che Guevara"* of Africa due to his revolutionary ideologies.

Sankara's parents wanted him to become a catholic priest, but he instead opted to join the military. During his military training, young Sankara met with Blaise Compaore, a man who shared the same revolutionary ideas and political beliefs as him. They became inseparable best friends and brothers. In 1970, at the age of 20, Sankara was sent to Madagascar for officer training where he witnessed a student popular uprising that led to the fall of the Madagascar government. Many experts believe that from that point on, a Sankara-led revolution was imminent. He became very good friends with a lot of revolutionary leaders around the world: Jerry Rawlings of Ghana, Fidel Castro of Cuba, Samora Machel of Mozambique, and so on. His political ideologies made him a threat to then President Ouedraogo's government which made him a political target, and he often got arrested and put into jail. On August 4, 1983, while serving a jail term, his best friend, and political comrade together with other military officers, overthrew Ouedraogo's government and freed Sankara from jail and appointed him as the leader of their revolution. Sankara cited rampant corruption, injustice, and poverty as the main reasons for toppling the former government.

When Sankara became the president, Upper Volta was poverty stricken; only 10% of the population was literate, with high infant mortality rate, and very low local food production. He made a lot of socialist reform policies; he nationalized a lot of private entities and implemented reforestation projects. He implemented programs that targeted elimination of corruption and poverty and improved education and food sufficiency. He made women empowerment one of the major priorities of his government which made many critics labeled him as a feminist. He prohibited female genital mutilation (FGM) and spoke enthusiastically against polygamy. He renamed the country to instill self-pride and unity among its 60 different ethnic groups. He called it Burkina Faso, *"The Land of Upright People"*, from the two major ethnic languages, Mossi and Dyula tribes.

Though loved by many, his ideas and policies were also considered as radicalized nationalism. Many public officials and political oppositions considered his decisions and actions as semi dictatorial. At the time of his death his monthly presidential salary was valued at $450 per month. His most valuable assets were a car, 4 bicycles, 3 guitars, a fridge, and a broken freezer. He led by example and expected his cabinet, government officials, and regular citizens to do the same. He sold all luxury Mercedes Benz vehicles belonging to government cabinet ministers and bought them low-maintenance vehicles. He prohibited government officials from flying first class while on government missions. And he implemented a policy of two meals a day with 10 liters of water per person for its citizens.

Sankara's ideas caused a lot of resentment toward him even from his closed political connects. His former Security Minister, Ernest Ouedraogo, reported that he remembered advising Sankara that his best friend and comrade, Blaise Compaore, was plotting to overthrow his government. And he said Sankara responded to him that if it was Blaise who is planning to overthrow his government then he has no defense against him. It is easy for one to defend him/herself from an external enemy, but how can one fight an enemy that is within, especially an enemy that one values as oneself?

On October 15th, 1987, in what came to be known as "*the great betrayal*" in Burkina Faso, Sankara was murdered in a coup led by his onetime best friend and brother, Blaise Compaore. He was in a meeting with his colleague, Traore Alouna, and two others. Alouna, who happened to be the only survivor of the attack, was believed to have played dead when the gunmen opened fire at them. He said when they first heard the sound of gunshots, Sankara told them to stay calm and remain inside and that it was him they came for. He walked outside with his hands up, which symbolized his surrendering to them, but the gunmen had already made up their minds; they shot him multiple times without any form of resistance from Sankara.

Few weeks before his death, during an anniversary remembrance of Che Guevara, Sankara was quoted saying that *"Revolutionaries and individuals can be murdered, but ideas never die"*. In October of 2014, Blaise Campaore's government was brought to its knees during a mass youth popular uprising led by a grassroots youth group, Le Balai Citoyen, *"Citizens Broom"*. Citizens were seen marching in the streets with the pictures of Sankara on sign boards. The movement was considered by many observers as the rising of the ghost of Sankara. Thomas Isidore Noel Sankara was a man with integrity and an incorruptible soul. The revolutionary man may have been killed, but his ideas are still alive in the land of Upright People and throughout Africa.

V. The Kenneth Kaunda Story:

The man known to many Zambians as *"the man with a big heart"* because of his generosity, Kenneth David Kaunda, is the founding father and the first President of Rhodesia, present day Zambia. This landlocked country in Southern Africa, home to the mighty Zambezi River and the Victoria Falls, has its capital city as Lusaka.

Kaunda was born on the 28th of April 1924 at Lubwa, near Chinali, Zambia. He is the son of a minister of the Church of Scotland in Zambia, Rev David Kaunda, and his mother was the first African woman to become a teacher in colonial Zambia. He has 8 children with his wife, Betty. In the mid 1940's like many Zambians during the colonial era Kaunda traveled to Tanganyika, present day Tanzania, to teach. He returned to Zambia in 1949 and became an interpreter and adviser on African affairs to Sir Stewart Gore-Browne, a colonial councilman. His closeness to the colonial lawmakers made him build interest in politics and become more politically conscious. This motivated him to join the first major anti-colonial organization in Zambia, African National Congress (ANC).

In the 1950's, Kaunda became the secretary general of the ANC party, but due to differences in ideology, he left and started his own party, Zambia African National Congress (ZNAC). He started a civil disobedience movement that he described as a *"Positive Nonviolent Action"* and generated a lot of grassroots support. His actions caught the attention of the colonial rulers, and he was arrested and sent to jail. This raised his political profile and made him a prominent candidate in the struggle for independence. He was released from jail on January 8th, 1960 and was selected to become the President of United National Independence Party (UNIP), a new party that was formed by his former ANC comrade, Mainza Chona, while he was jailed. His popularity grew bigger and he became an international icon. In 1960, he visited Martin Luther King Jr. in the U.S. to seek for support and to strengthen his non-violent advocacy for independence.

On October 1st, 1964, Kaunda ushered Zambia into independence. At the time Zambia had 73 different indigenous tribes plus foreign settlers, Pakistanis, English, Welsh, Indians, and Scottish, which he had the responsibility to shape into *"One Zambia and One Nation"*. On his independence inauguration speech, he spoke of the new republic, *"task of building a nation founded on respect for all people of all races, all colors and all religions"*. He freed 200 freedom fighters that were charged with sedition and jailed by the colonial government. He instituted an educational policy to provide school supplies for all school children. He shared Kwame Nkrumah's vision of independent Africa. He supported liberation movements in Mozambique, Angola, South Africa, Namibia, Guinea Bissau, and so many other countries.

Like many other independent African governments, Kaunda was faced with many post-independence issues including tribalism. He was able to maintain stability through very difficult times in Zambia's history. A huge tribal and political violence broke out in the Zambia's 1968 elections. In response, he banned all political parties in 1972, except for his own party (UNIP). Like Nkrumah of Ghana, and Nyerere of Tanzania, he too ruled Zambia with a one-party state until the democratic waves that were sweeping through the continent washed his government away in the early 1990's.

Many Zambians criticized his government at the time for focusing on and investing too many resources on copper mining for exports and neglecting agriculture and food production. While copper exportations were high, Zambia became too dependent on food importation and foreign aid. When the price of copper fell in the world market in the late 80's, the Zambian economy went on a downward spiral. Faced with the increase in public dissatisfaction and political oppositions, coupled with tribalism and high unemployment rate, Kaunda was forced to lift the ban on political parties in 1990. On November 2nd, 1991, he lost Zambia's first multi-party elections to Frederick Chiluba, leader of the Movement for Multiparty Democracy (MMD). This led many observers to question his popularity since the first real test of his popularity ended in a defeat for his government.

Kenneth David Kaunda continued to serve as the president of his party until the year 2000. In March of 1999, he was stripped of his Zambian citizenship by the then government based on a clause in the Zambian constitution that declares that citizenship is attain by heritance and not by birth; his parents were originally from Malawi. That was a very unfortunate and embarrassing event in Zambia's history. Later in the year 2000, he was declared a Zambian citizen by a Supreme Court decision. Kaunda is officially retired from public office and as of this writing, focuses on charity work and social activism. He is a huge advocate of HIV and AIDS awareness; his first son died of the virus.

VI. The Jomo Kenyatta Story:

Kenya, which is believed to have derived its name from Mount Kenya, which means *"God's Resting Place"* from the Embu and Kamba tribes, has its capital city as Nairobi. Nairobi is one of the fastest growing cities in Africa. Kenya is home to some of the best long-distance (Olympic) marathon runners in the world today and encompasses some of Africa's wildest animals and savannahs. Kenya was once a British colony until the 12th of December 1963, when Jomo Kenyatta, the man known to his people as *"Mzee"*, elderly person in Swahili, became the first president of Kenya.

Mzee was born in 1891, in Ichaweri village, British East Africa, present day Kenya. He was the son of a leader of the Kikuyu agricultural settlement, Ngengi. Kenyatta was a man with resolve and initiatives. He put himself through school by working for a white settler as a houseboy. After he completed his studies, he moved to Nairobi, where he became a clerk in the public works department, and adopted the name Kenyatta, a term in the Kikuyu term for a fancy belt he normally wore. Kenya had a caste system during the colonial days based on a color bar. Whites were first-class citizens, Asian were second-class, and blacks were third-class citizens in their own motherland. This injustice and many others prompted Kenyatta to advocate for self-rule.

He began his political advocacy when he joined an East African Association (EAA) who were fighting to reclaim Kikuyu lands that were leased to British settlers in 1920, when Kenya became a British crown colony. In 1929, Kenyatta travelled to the UK to advocate for the land rights of the Kikuyu people and to speak against a scheme that the colony had designed to join Kenya, Uganda, and Tanzania as one territory. During his visit he wrote five recommendations to the secretary of state for British colonies. He recommended for lands allocated to Europeans to be returned to the Kikuyu people. Increase education amenities and opportunities for the indigenous people. Repeal hut taxes levied on poor women (especially widows). Include Africans in the legislative council, and noninterference of European Settlers into Africans' traditions and ways of life. These things Kenyatta recommended and advised that their failure to be adhered to can lead to *"dangerous explosion—the one thing all sane men wish to avoid"*. In 1952, his prophecy would come to light.

Kenyatta also played an integral part in the planning and organizing of the 5th Pan African Congress in England, which was also attended by Kwame Nkrumah, in 1945. Upon his return in 1947, he joined Kenya's struggle for self-rule. He championed a non-violence route to independence. In 1952, he was arrested and jailed for 7 years with hard labor, and accused of leading an indigenous rebel movement, called the *"Mau Mau"*, who were fighting for independence, charges Mzee denied. On his release in 1961, his followers and support base got even bigger and stronger.

In 1963, Kenya had its first multiparty elections and Kenyatta became its first prime minister. Hence the path to independence was paved. Threatened by the emergence of a black African President, the minority white settlers requested audience with Kenyatta to discuss their fate in the new Nation. His four-team advisory council advised him to give the settlers a probationary period to leave Kenya. Kenyatta instead went onto the podium and called for tolerance and cooperation between blacks and none-blacks for a better future for Kenya.

Like many founding fathers of many African countries, Kenyatta had opposition from his own countrymen too. As the oppositions grew more disgruntled, Kenyatta grew more intolerant. He amended the constitution to extend his powers. His one-time ally and former vice president, Jaramogi Ajuma Oginga Odinga, sets up an opposition party against his regime. Due to increase in political rivalry and tensions, Odinga's party was banned and he was arrested. This left Kenya as a one-party state in 1969 like many other African countries during that era. Like Ghana and Tanzania, Kenya also implemented the *"detention act"*, which allows opposition members to be arrested and detained without charges. Land issues and tribal aggressions began to rise across the nation. In July 1969, Tom Mboya, a potential presidential candidate was gunned down in Nairobi and his death came 4 years after another critic of Kenyatta's government, Pio Gama Pinto, was killed under similar circumstances. And again in 1975, Kariuki Mwangi, another politician against Kenyatta's government was also assassinated. Corruption and tribal favoritism became the order of the day in Kenya.

Many sympathizers of Kenyatta reported that a lot of the atrocities took place without his knowledge. It was said that Kenyatta grew too ill, and it was his close associates and government officials who were making decisions. It was reported that at some point in his presidency he was only a symbolic leader. He had become too old and sick to make executive decisions.

In August of 1978, in his late eighties, Kenyatta died in his sleep at his home. He is remembered for breaking the colonial legacy and instilling self-pride and belief in the heart of the Kenyan people. His close associates describe him as a kind-hearted man with a quick temper. Today Kenya continues to be the natural economic leader of East Africa, but it is still faced with ethnic divisions and tribalism.

VII. The Haile Selassie Story:

The story of Ethiopia's great monarch, modernizer, and arguable hero, Haile Selassie, began in a thousand-years-old city Harar. It was in this city that Rastafa, as he was commonly known, began his political crusade.

Haile Selassie was Ethiopia's 225th and last emperor. He was born on July 23rd, 1892, at Ejersa Goro, Ethiopia. His father Ras Makonnen, the governor of Harar, originally called him Ly Tafari Makonnen. At a very early age, his father decided to educate young Rastafa with tutors of various backgrounds, an Ethiopian catholic monk and a Mexican sergeant. Upon his father's demise in 1908, his elder brother, Dejazmach Yilma Makonnen, inherited his position as a governor. But his elder brother died an untimely death only 2 years later. Young Rastafa became the governor at 14 years old. At the age of 24 he was appointed as regent by his father's cousin, Emperor Menelik. In 1911, he married Wayzaro Menen, a great granddaughter of Menelik, and they had 6 children. He would later become the emperor of his state when Menelik passed away. Upon his coronation as emperor, his name was changed to Haile Selassie, *"Power of the Trinity"*, in the Amharic language. Some historians argue that he is a direct descendent of Queen Sheba and King Solomon, but there is no tangible evidence to support such claims.

When he became the emperor, Selassie moved from Harar to Addis Ababa, the capital city of Ethiopia. There were 11,000 people living in Addis Ababa, a city without any meaningful infrastructure at the time. He was able to unite the 83 different tribes within his kingdom using the influence of the church and being an advocate for tradition. During his time as emperor he visited over 167 different countries around the world. Some of his critics regarded him as very wasteful and flamboyant. However, the young emperor made the modernization and globalization of Ethiopia his main political agenda. In 1923, Ethiopia became the first African nation to join the League of Nations, present day United Nations. And in 1931, he drafted a constitution that many of his critics regarded as a dictatorial document because the constitution puts much of the power in his hands.

In 1936, Italy decided to invade Ethiopia, an action that caused a global outcry and condemnation around the world. Emperor Selassie traveled to the League of Nations to lobby for support on behalf of his nation. He was quoted saying *"it is my country today and yours tomorrow"*, but he failed to convince the League of Nations to come to his country's defense. The Italians invaded Ethiopia, captured its largest church, murdered over 300 monks and priests, and captured Addis Ababa. Emperor Selassie was forced into exile to the United Kingdom for five years, until 1941. The British soldiers together with local freedom fighters, invaded Ethiopia in January of 1941 and recaptured Addis Ababa from the Italians. Haile Selassie was welcomed back home to once again ascend to his throne and reunite his disfranchised kingdom into one Ethiopia.

Upon his return, Selassie used some of the ideas and techniques he learned while he was in exile in England. His drive to modernize Ethiopia was done with urgency and precision. His first order of business was to build schools and institutions. He made education his kingdom's priority and personally served as the minister of education for many years. He built Ethiopia's first university and many secondary schools. He groomed local educators to replace foreign teachers. He built Ethiopia's first airline and strongly promoted tourism and trade. Today Ethiopia continues to benefit from some of his economic policies. In 2012, Ethiopian Airlines had total revenue of 42 million dollars, which is more than a quarter of many other African countries' annual GDP.

Emperor Selassie was worshipped in his time like a demigod, and the followers of the Rastafarian spirituality hailed him as a prophet. He became Africa's biggest champion in 1963, when he invited Nkrumah of Ghana and Mwalimu of Tanzania, together with 31 other African leaders to Addis Ababa. It was during this gathering that the Organization of African Unity (OAU), present day African Union (AU), was founded. He took a personal interest in promoting self-rule and the struggle to end colonialism within the African continent and he also served as a peace negotiator between many African countries.

The majority of the land in Ethiopia then, like many other monarchs with feudal systems, belonged to the nobility and the royal class. With socialism and Marxism gaining popularity around the world, this didn't sit well with the indigenous people of Ethiopia. Socialist drums began to vibrate from all corners of his kingdom. In the early seventies, famine, unemployment, and land reform issues also began to create more opposition against the throne. In 1974, a mutiny broke out within his army that paved the way for other rebellions. His kingdom was overthrown by a Marxist socialist rebel group, the Derg, under the leadership of Mengistu Haile Mariam. They targeted the monarchy and arrested his Majesty. Some of his family members were arrested and detained for 14 years while many fled to neighboring countries. The emperor himself was given the ultimate penalty, death. His cause of death is still unknown, but many believe that he was strangled.

VIII. The Patrice Lumumba Story:

Congo, the richest country on earth in terms of natural resources and yet the poorest in terms of GDP, has a population of over 75 million people with over 240 different tribes/languages. However, no son/daughter of its land is more talked about or celebrated as Patrice Lumumba.

Patrice Lumumba was born Elias Okit'Asombo on July 2, 1925, in Onalua Village, Belgian Congo, present day Democratic Republic of Congo. His parents were Francois Tolenga Otetshima, Dad, and Julienne Wamato Lomendja, Mom. In 1951, he married his first wife, Pauline Opangu. They had five children, Francois (the oldest), Patrice Junior, Julienne, Roland, and Guy-Patrice Lumumba.

After completing high school at a Protestant mission-
ary school and a one-year post office training school, he
moved to Leopoldville, present day Kinshasa, and worked
as a postal clerk and later became an accountant at the post
office in the mid 1940's. In 1956, Lumumba, alongside other African Belgian Congolese went on a tour of Belgium under the supervision of the then minister of colonies. Upon
his return back to Congo, he was arrested and charged with
embezzling the postal service funds and sentenced to a 12
months jailed term. Charges that many observers believe
were the beginning of organized propagandas to tarnish
the young revolutionary leader's image.

Early in his life he became a formidable leader in organizing unions and advocacy groups, this gained him major acclaims and recognitions. In 1958, he co-founded the
Mouvement National Congolais (MNC), the organization
called for a national unity among all 242 different tribes of
Congo to bring an end to colonial misrule. In 1959, he was
arrested for instigating and championing an anti-colonial
riot in Stanleyville that left 30 people dead and was sentenced to 69 months in prison. His incarceration coincided
with a roundtable political discussion between local political parties and the colonial rulers that was scheduled to
take place in Brussels. His party, the MNC, refused to grace
the occasion without the attendance of their party leader.
This occasion forced the colonial government to release Lumumba and allowed him to attend the Brussels conference.

*"For this independence of the Congo, even as it is celebrated
today with Belgium, a friendly country with whom we deal as
equal to equal, no Congolese worthy of the name will ever be
able to forget that it was by fighting that it has been won, a day*

to day fight, an ardent and idealistic fight, a fight in which we
were spared neither privation nor suffering, and for which we
gave our strength and our blood. We are proud of this struggle,
of tears, of fire, and of blood, to the depths of our being, for it
was a noble and just struggle, and indispensable to put an end
to the humiliating slavery which was imposed upon us by force"

EXCERPT FROM PATRICE LUMUMBA
INDEPENDENCE SPEECH IN 1960.

Young 35-year-old Lumumba led Congo to independence on June 30th, 1960. His independence speech highlighted the injustice, oppression, and exploitation of the Congolese under the Belgian colonial government. His speech was considered highly offensive and disrespectful towards King Baudouin of Belgium who was in attendance.

As the new Prime Minister of Congo, Lumumba raised the salary of all the government employees except for that of the army. After twelve weeks of independence, his national honeymoon period wouldn't last long before it was interrupted by infighting among his comrades with support from outside influence. The then president, Joseph Kasa-Vubu dismissed Lumumba from his official position as prime minister. Lumumba also in retaliation declared Kasa-Vubu out of office in a vote of no confidence in the Congolese senate. This incident left Congo as one nation with two political groups claiming legitimacy as governors. His one-time revolutionary ally turned opposition, Moise Tshombe took advantage of the confusion, and backed a small disgruntled section of the army, and proclaimed that the mineral rich region of Congo, Katanga, was separating from Congo. The Belgians sent in their troops to rescue

Chapter Five

their citizens during the confusion and coincidentally, or rather strategically, settled in and re-occupied Katanga and supported the Moise Tshombe led rebel group in the mineral rich region. Lumumba called upon the United Nations to help convince/expel the Belgian troops out of Congo in order to restore internal order but was faced with similar fate to that of King Selassie of Ethiopia during the Italian invasion. The UN ignored his call. Congo, a newly independent African nation in its infant stages trying to rise from the ashes of the brutal colonial regime, couldn't do much on its own to bring an end to the Belgian-backed rebel group of Katanga. Left with no other choice, Lumumba turned to the Soviet Union that was at the time involved in a Cold War with the World Superpowers, America. Lumumba's foreign policy decisions were viewed by America and its allies as irresponsible and sabotaging towards American interest. Lumumba was labeled as a communist sympathizer and was caught in the Cold War crossfire. Unfortunately for him, he became a mere collateral damage in a war that had nothing to do with Congo or Africa.

"Neither brutality, nor cruelty nor torture will ever bring me to ask for mercy, for I prefer to die with my head unbowed, my faith unshakable and with profound trust in the destiny of my country, rather than live under subjection and disregarding sacred principles. History will one day have its say, but it will not be the history that is taught in Brussels, Paris, Washington, or the United Nations, but the history which will be taught in the countries dread from imperialism and its puppets. Africa will write its own history, and to the north and south of the Sahara, it will be a glorious and dignified history. Do not weep

for me, my dear wife. I know that my country, which is suffer-
ing so much, will know how to defend its independence and its
liberty. Long live the Congo! Long live Africa!"
EXCERPT FROM PATRICE LUMUMBA LAST LETTER TO HIS
FIRST WIFE BEFORE HIS EXECUTION. PUBLISHED ON
NEW AFRICA WEBSITE ON 01/18/2018.

Lumumba was captured by his own military command-er, Joseph Mobutu, and taken to Katanga where he was shot dead while tied to a tree together with two of his new-ly appointed ministers, Maurice Mpolo and Joseph Okito, on January 17th, 1961. Their bodies were dissolved in sul-phuric acid. The U.S.A. (CIA), Belgium, and England where all implicated in Lumumba's death. Larry Delvin, Head of CIA in Congo during Lumumba's murder confessed that U.S. President Dwight Eisenhower orders the CIA to "*elim-inate*" him.

Lumumba's ideologies and revolutionary principles were not any different from his fellow Pan-Africans at the time. He called for a united Congo irrespective of tribal or political affiliation. He advocated for an Africa that will be governed by Africans for Africans based on African values. His believes were motivated by nothing other than his Af-rican pride. He was branded as a huge threat to western in-terest, especially during the times when the battles of the minds where at their highest. Lumumba's death generated an international outcry both within the African continent and around the world. Even his murderers labeled him as a "*national hero*".

The purpose of writing this chapter is not to sanitize or taint the image of some of the greatest inaugural leaders of our continent. The fact of the matter is that the majority of all the inaugural leaders of our continent are all dead and gone. But my concern is, have we learned from their mistakes? Have we prepared enough young leaders to succeed them? I would like for us to remember certain peculiar things from the lives of these great men as we move forward as a continent. Learn from the life of Kwame Nkrumah and hear him say *"we face neither east nor west, we face forward"*. Listen to Nkrumah and face forward with one vision united under one God and purpose. Learn from the life of Julius Nyerere and hear him say *"independence cannot be real if a nation depends upon gifts"*. Listen to Nyerere and let us liberate and economically emancipate our continent. We cannot grow by depending on *"gifts"*. Learn from the life of Nelson Mandela and hear him say *"I dream of an Africa which is in peace with itself"*. Listen to Mandela and stop inflicting pain on ourselves with endless wars, corruptions, and bad governance. Let us be at peace with ourselves. Learn from the life of Thomas Sankara and hear him say *"Land of the Upright People"*. Listen to Sankara and act like we are not the children of a lesser God or lesser beings, but that we are the children of *"Upright People"*. Learn from the life of Patrice Lumumba and hear him say *"Africa will write its own history, and it will be, to the north and to the south of the Sahara, a history of glory and dignity"*. Listen to Lumumba and do not despair for the simple fact that we know our continent shall rise again and the history of the resurgence of our continent shall be written by the sons and daughters of our land. Learn from the life of King Haile Selassie and hear him say *"an awareness of our past is essential to the establishment and our identity as Africans"*. Listen to Selassie and let us revisit our history and build diverse democracies that would be representative of our African norms and values, and if our values coincide with western values then so be it, but we must be true to ourselves. Learn from the life of Jomo Kenyatta and hear him say *"our children may learn about the heroes of the past. Our task is to make ourselves the architects of the future"*. Listen to Kenyatta and understand that Africa will remain a low voltage contributor in world affairs unless our engineers become problem solvers, our doctors become healers, our politicians become accountable to our people, our farmers become nation feeders, our youths become nation builders, our women become the custodians of our society, our lawyers become defenders of justice, and our uniformed men and women become our protectors and crusaders. And finally, learn from Kenneth Kaunda and hear him say *"there are numerous reasons why African leaders need to be more strategic in cultivating a relationship with the Diaspora"*. Hear Kaunda and understand that the renaissance and resurgence of the African continent is a collective pluralism that needs to include the contribution of all Africans irrespective of ethnicity, tribe, or political affiliation, both home and abroad. We have a responsibility and in fact a duty to build our continent.

Outro

Will the respective African countries realize their full potential and be truly independent one day? I am 100% certain of the possibility that African countries can be truly independent one day. Other parts of the world have been independent economically, politically, culturally, socially, and so forth for many decades if not centuries. Of course, the process has been gradual, but today looking at what they have achieved, one can rightly confirm that they are relatively independent. In many regards, their citizens make their own choices about the way they live, are led, or are treated by their leaders, or even by the rest of the world. And there are no fundamental reasons why African countries cannot reach that same level of self-realization and independence. We have seen a success story with Cape Verde, effective January of 2008, Cape Verde graduated from being a Least Developed Country (LDC) to a Middle-Income Country (MIC). They attained this via stable currency pegged to the Euro, good governance with low corruption rate, a simplified tax system, and a reformed banking sector. Other African countries can use similar models to improve the livelihood of their people. I am not very thrilled with the idea of pegging our currencies against western currencies, but we must start somewhere. Botswana, the longest standing democracy of the continent, is another encouraging story. We have even seen Rwanda emerging as the technological hub of the continent. I foresee a continent where we will have economic integrations and merge our diverse currencies that we can peg against our natural resources in our soils.

All civilizations that existed in the history of time defined clear agendas and purpose that all their people worked to attain. Africa needs her own defined dreams and agenda that all her people can strive to achieve with a single collective purpose; building our continent. WE HAVE A CONTINENT TO BUILD.

Acknowledgement

I am grateful to God for my good health and wellbeing that were necessary to complete this book. I wish to express my sincere thanks to my mother, Aja Sarata Ceesay, my confidante and best friend for always believing in me. And my father, Alagie Alieu Camara, who even in death continues to be my biggest motivating factor. We did it again Baba; we are now on our second book.

Nobody has been more important in my pursuit of perpetual growth today than you my daughter, Asiya Kaddy Camara. You have become my biggest inspiration and I love you. I equally wish to thank my loving and supportive family, Kaddy, Nyaling, Aminata, Baboucarr, Ibrahim, Kalifa, Kabiru, Baba Saikou, Yankuba, and Alpha, who provide unending support and inspiration.

Justice Haddy Roche, thank you for making valuable comments and suggestions on this project which gave me an inspiration to improve the quality of the content and for keeping me honest throughout my writing process.

"Prima Facie", my sister and friend, Mrs. Cany Jobe-Taal, thank you for continuing to be my cheerleader and encourager. You always find a way to bring the best out of me. Whether it is via an energetic and animated debate or via motivating and uplifting words, you always find the right words to light the fire within me. Thank you for your friendship.

Thank you to Mr. Jamal Drammeh and Mr. Ebou Cham, you two have introduced me to new perspectives on the subject matter. Your passion for the subject matter is evident and highly appreciated.

I would also like to expand my sincere gratitude to Valerie Bourdain, Melvin Foote, Dr. Julius W. Garvey, and all those who have directly and indirectly guided me in completing this book.

About the Author

Saikou is an international motivational speaker and a seasoned storyteller. As an African, storytelling is part of his culture and it plays an instrumental part in his life. He perceives storytelling as an art form that links us to our past and gives us foresight into the future. He has been invited to speak at the United Nations, De Montfort University (Leicester City, UK), Bowie State University, Virginia Tech, RightsCon (Brussels), Portland University, University of the Gambia, Omaha YP Summit, among others. He is also the author of "Testimony of An African Immigrant—A Promise to My Father."

Saikou Camara is from West Africa, the Gambia. He traveled to the United States in 2004 to go to school. He graduated with his BS in Computer Science from Rust College (2008), in Holly Springs, Mississippi and graduated with his master's Degree, in Computer Science, from Jackson State University (2010), in Jackson Mississippi.

Saikou is the founder and the President of Your Change for a Change (YCFaC), a 501C3 non-profit organization incorporated in the state of Nebraska and registered in five different countries (USA, The Gambia, UK, Sweden, and France). He is the President of a non-profit organization, People Making a Difference (PMaD,) incorporated in the state of Nebraska (2014), comprising of mainly young African professionals within the greater Omaha area. Saikou is currently serving as a board member for the Simple Foundation incorporated in Omaha Nebraska. As an activist with a passion for youth empowerment, Saikou co-founded the Global Leadership Empowerment and Diversity Summit (GLEADS) in 2016, which brings together diverse group of young leaders to discuss innovative ideas and find solutions to our everyday challenges facing our diverse communities.

Saikou now draws from his experience as a trained IT professional and president for non-profit organizations to provide Project Development Consultancy for many start-up businesses and entrepreneurs especially in the fields of technology and not-for-profit.

He was awarded the Superior Community Service award by the Black Employee Network (BEN) in 2014, and the Citizen of The Year award two years in a row, 2015-2016, by the Beta Upsilon Chapter of Omega Psi Phi Fraternity Incorporated.